"No one is a more convincing advocate of the gospel than a man deeply in love with the Savior, his Word and his world. JD Wetterling is such a man, and writes with a passion for each that no one can miss, nor should."

Dr. Bryan Chapell, President,
Covenant Theology Seminary, St. Louis, Missouri

"The first time I read something that JD Wetterling had written – a guest column in The Wall Street Journal – I knew I had to get to know this man better. Indeed, because what he said in those few words was so compelling, I picked up the phone and called him, even though I'd never heard of him before. JD Wetterling knew then – and he still knows – how to capture the biggest ideas in life in a few arresting words, and he does that wonderfully in this little book. He's the kind of writer who makes you yearn to sit down and talk some more with him after you've finished reading what he wrote."

Joel Belz, founder of World magazine

"JD Wetterling clearly explains six key verses from the gospel of John that all Christians should take to heart. He emphasizes God's sovereignty and the assurance that deepens among all those who fully trust in Him."

Marvin Olasky, editor-in-chief,
World magazine and author

"Once again JD Wetterling has opened a door that I was afraid to open. For forty years I kept the door closed on the Vietnam event – two tours, 500 hours of air combat, medals and all that. I wanted to forget it and just get on with my life. But JD opened that door in *Son of Thunder* so I could deal with the reality of war and accept myself again. Now, in *No one...* he has opened another door, the courage to speak publicly about my faith. This little book will always be my companion when I travel to world mission fields. I am frequently asked to speak extemporaneously and now I have a ready text with a message for all peoples and all occasions. Thanks, JD."

Terry Kennedy, Executive Director of Serve

"In a world that repeatedly questions the divinity of Christ and His truthful words comes a refreshing work from JD Wetterling that addresses the very essence of what each believer and seeker should know about a relationship with the Savior. As a Pastor, I highly recommend this dynamic book as an affirmation for the follower of Jesus and as a evangelistic tool in reaching others for Him. *No one...* is for everyone who seeks a heart connection with Christ!"

Dr. Bert Welch, Pastor,
Covenant Baptist Church (SBC),
Lancaster, South Carolina

"When life is shaken down to its most essential properties, when we are confronted with life and death choices, what becomes most important? In his forceful book, *No one...*, JD Wetterling touches on the essential issues and questions that challenge us to make sense of life for the present as well as for eternity. JD writes like he lives: straight and honest, with a spirit of concern for everyone's eternal destiny. He flew many missions as a combat pilot, but none were as important to him as the one he has set out in this book. Now he is fighting for the souls of men and women to know the certainty of life, which is true and eternal. And he does this by pointing us all to Jesus Christ, the only Savior who can and does secure eternal life for all who believe."

Dr. Dominic Aquila,
President, New Geneva Theological Seminary,
Colorado Springs, Colorado

"Compared to many, this is a small book! You will find, however, its message towering above many other things you have read. Its magnitude is established by its simple and profound wording, readability, clear thinking, solid content, straight-forward style, and the dependability of really good theology grounded in the authority of God's word. I am thankful for the opportunity to commend *No one...* to you. Each time I have read it, I have wondered to myself, why hasn't someone said this before? It is so right! I am confident that you will find it a helpful apologetic and evangelistic tool. I am confident that you will also find it refreshing and restorative to your own certainty in the face of many uncertainties."

Rev. Mo Up De Graff, Administrator,
Ridge Haven Conference Center and Retreat

"This is a short book but a powerful book showing the reality of the gospel and also the power of the gospel. You will do well to read it and also to pass along to others. It will strengthen the faith of believers and lead others to consider the claims of Christ in a very real and practical way."

Paul D. Kooistra, Coordinator,
Mission to the World

"You, like me, probably are often casting about for a readable booklet to put into the hands of a thoughtful, unconverted acquaintance. JD Wetterling has provided such a tool for us. Mr. Wetterling writes clearly and persuasively about six exclusive claims of Jesus Christ. Because ours is a time in which people place the highest premium on toleration, it is necessary to confront them with the exclusive claims of Jesus Christ. I plan on keeping copies with me, as I travel, to give to people who show an interest in talking about the gospel of Jesus Christ."

Dr. Joseph A. Pipa Jr., President,
Greenville Presbyterian Theological Seminary,
Greenville, South Carolina

"In our day there is a mad search for reality and certainty – even in the church. Therefore we Christians must be explicit in all our God-talk because we are all sinners and need a Savior. *No one...* points clearly and directly to the ONE – Jesus – who accomplishes salvation for His people. It enables us to see and savor Jesus Christ, the fullest and most beautiful manifestation of the glory of God. It is a great instrument for youth and adults to get them grounded and encouraged in the truth of a relationship with Jesus Christ."

**The Rev. R. Grady Love, Retired Pastor,
Brevard, North Carolina**

"JD Wetterling has given us nothing less than the gospel in all its simplicity, beauty and glory. If this message is news to you, read this book and let God speak to your soul. If this is news you have heard a thousand times, allow yourself to hear it again, and let your faith be strengthened and renewed."

**Tim Challies,
uber God-blogger at challies.com**

"It is rare that an author can discuss the simplicity of the gospel along side its intricacies; rarer still when he can present the works of God in his sovereignty in such a winsome way. JD Wetterling has accomplished both of these tasks. Applicable to seekers as well as mature believers, this is a tool for evangelism as well as an aid on the path to spiritual maturity."

Dr. Dan H. Youngren, Trimont, Minnesota

"Are you searching for encouragement in this uncertain world and want reassurance that God is in charge? In *No one...*, JD Wetterling describes God's gracious plan of redemption in a concise manner, bringing understanding and confirmation of God's faithfulness. I have received Evangelism Explosion training and find this book helpful to all who present the gospel to others."

Jim Hassinger, Elder, Columbia, Missouri

"In a clear an uncompromising manner, JD Wetterling writes about six certainties set forth by the Word. He is clear, concise and highlights that truth is not up for grabs but based on absolutes that assure us of the trustworthiness of God's Word. This book exalts the Lord, his written Word, and the absolute truths that undergird our Christian faith."

Charles Dunahoo,
Coordinator of Christian Education & Publications,
Presbyterian Church in America (PCA)

"JD Wetterling is right on target. In a book that can be read in a couple of hours, the absolute truth of the Bible is presented in a compelling manner. This is a must read for the seeker and will be enjoyed by every believer as they are refreshed again with their salvation."

The Rev. Mack Griffith, Chaplain, US Army

"JD Wetterling presents, in concise, solid, theologically clear language six fundamental pillars of our Christian faith for the new, the casual, and the mature believer. It is food for the soul that contributes to a mature balanced diet that all should taste and savor."

Bill Newton, Pastor,
Woodland Hills Baptist Church, Asheville,
North Carolina

"JD has written a book that gives a solid foundation of truths on which to build your life. How to personally know God, how to walk with Him, and how to view all of life in the light of this – what more important issues can be considered? I highly recommend this book!"

Dr. Frank M. Barker, Jr., Pastor Emeritus,
Briarwood Presbyterian Church, Birmingham, Alabama

"No one..."

When Jesus says it, he means it

Strange, my soul, is it not?
All men are negligent of their souls
till grace gives them reason,
then they leave their madness
and act like rational beings,
but not till then.

Charles H. Spurgeon

****

"No one..."

When Jesus says it, he means it

JD Wetterling

CHRISTIAN FOCUS

© JD Wetterling, 2006
www.jdwetterling.com

ISBN 1-84550-153-5
ISBN 978-1-84550-153-2

10 9 8 7 6 5 4 3 2 1

Published in 2006
by
Christian Focus Publications, Ltd.
Geanies House, Fearn, Tain,
Ross-shire, IV20 1TW, Scotland, UK
www.christianfocus.com

Cover design by Danie Van Straaten
Printed and bound by Nørhaven Paperback A/S

Contents

Preface

The world will never forget the tragedy of September 11, 2001, when 2,800 innocent people died in the twin towering infernos of the World Trade Center, my former home office in New York City. The visual images are so horrifying the human mind does not want to remember, let alone contemplate them. Yet one picture, of the many indelibly imprinted on my gray matter, refuses to recede from my conscious mind. It is a still photo of a man falling from one of the burning towers. He is just one of about seventy people who chose to jump to their death rather than be consumed by the fire. Just trying to imagine the thought process of that decision, in the chaos and terror of the moment, is so painful the mind refuses to process it.

The man in the photo, unlike the others that I saw, was not tumbling as he fell. I witnessed his fall real time and in the videotape as it was replayed that day. He was falling headfirst, straight down with perfect posture, arms at his sides with one knee bent as if he was about to take a step. That is not a normal way for the human body to fall. In my adventurous youth when I was learning to skydive, my body was all somersaulting ankles and elbows until I learned to fall in a controlled manner, and it was not straight down headfirst. The profile view of the man was not close enough to see his face, but there is a strong sense of serenity exuded by his body language just seconds before his instantaneous death. And that is what consumes me. Did he know his eternal destiny? Did he have the blessed assurance of his salvation? Were millions of us witnessing the death of a saint?

If so, it was the second time for me. My saintly mother, who was my mentor in all the important lessons of living and dying, breathed her last with a serenity that was an overwhelming witness to her faith for her assembled family. She was wired up and kept alive by the machinery of modern medicine and could not sing, but she mouthed all her favorite hymns we sang at her bedside. Her last whispered words to me were, "I am almost there." I wonder if the falling man knew he was "almost there" and was in fact taking his first step into eternity with the Lord God Almighty, even as he fell.

Another thing about this tragedy I've pondered at length: many of those 2,800 people who were not instantly killed were trapped in the top floors of the towers. They had from thirty minutes to an hour in which imminent death was a certainty. We know from phone calls to loved ones that was so. We also know that there were a number of godly people among them who perhaps witnessed to them. As a novel writer I spend a lot of time trying to put myself inside the head of other people and inject myself into scenes I can only imagine. I wonder how many of them were spiritually born again in the last hour of their life. I want to believe many of them were. Hopefully those desperate men and women, knowing no other options remained, fought off the mental paralysis of fear and fell on their knees even as they felt the heat of the flames, the shuddering of the building and finally the floor giving way beneath them. I hope and pray they asked for forgiveness for their sins, begged a merciful God to admit them into paradise that day as they claimed the covering blood of Christ. In my experience as a combat fighter pilot I learned the wonderfully focusing effect that imminent death has on the mind. We can be sure those who prayed in their final hour had no problems with wandering minds, insincerity in their pleas for mercy or lack of intensity in their cries for salvation. God most likely gathered a number of his children in the last moments of the World Trade Center's existence.

By God's mercy, believers and unbelievers alike died with a minimum of pain, unlike the millions of people who suffer for long periods of time with the diseases that ravage humankind. But their greatest blessing was that they had the opportunity to get right with their Maker and Savior before they died. How many people today are banking on seeing death coming and getting prepared at the last minute? How many think they want to enjoy their life of sin and selfishness, have a deathbed conversion, then spend eternity in paradise? Dear reader, such depravity plays Russian roulette with your eternal soul. Many, both the damned and the redeemed, died instantly when the airliners hit the World Trade Center, but the wail of the damned will sound forever as they are eternally consumed in "the fiery furnace" (Matt. 13:42).

As a child I believed in Santa Claus, the tooth fairy and Jesus Christ. Fifty years of life experiences, Bible reading, comparative religion studies including evolution theories, and I still believe in Jesus, now with an informed conviction – head knowledge and heart knowledge.

Some folks have never known him except as a common curse word. For others he disappeared from their worldview soon after Santa and the tooth fairy. If the polls are correct, a majority of people who call themselves Christian think Jesus has no more relevance than Santa. They are lost and oblivious to their "lostness."

The latter category I call casual Christians. They know what is needed for salvation but just procrastinate when it comes to acting on it. Next Sunday I will go to church. ... As soon as I get past this big project at the office I will find time for daily devotions. ... I suspect the majority of souls in hell fall into this category. They simply put off asking God to change their hearts one day too long. A significant number of those who perished in the top stories of the north tower of the World Trade Center died not knowing what hit them. Those who die from terrorist bombings around the world do not see it coming. People die suddenly every day. In 2001, 41,730 Americans died in auto accidents, 93,000 in other accidents, 15,000 were murdered, 160,000 died from strokes, 700,000 died from heart disease, many of them instantly.

Life is uncertain, as the terrorist attack of 9/11 so graphically demonstrated. "No man knows when his hour will come" (Eccl. 9:12a) – the hour that God determined before we were born. The Psalmist says, "All the days ordained for me were written in your book before one of them came to be" (Ps. 139:16b). That same Holy Writ contains the only certainty there is in an uncertain world. In spite of so much evil, so much hatred and so little love for the God who made us all, there are some unshakable certainties we can cling to in this unstable powder keg called planet Earth.

This little book is an effort on the part of a sinner saved by grace to witness to the power of a handful of the most important of them. They are unshakable certainties that can, God willing, open your eyes to his truth, fill you with the peace that transcends all understanding, and show you the way to the unimaginable joy of life, both now and forever, with him.

One of my favorite newspaper columnists, the late Mike Royko, wrote, on the sudden death of his wife, "If there is someone you love and have not said it lately, do it now. Always, always, do it now." In the same manner, if you have not asked God to change your heart, do it now. Always, always do it now. God willing, the following words of Jesus who saves can save you too.

Introduction

The Gospel of John contains six things certain and unshakable that can change your life. They are six sayings for the ages, six profound revelations of God's truth from the Son of God's own lips.

What Jesus Christ said counts forever. He is not a figment of someone's imagination. He was a real figure in the history of mankind. We have more historical proof that he lived than for any other person of antiquity. The miracle of his resurrection from the dead, witnessed by hundreds besides his inner circle of disciples, capped a brief lifetime of miracles witnessed by thousands that verified he was who he repeatedly claimed to be – the Son of God. In his own words, "I and the Father are one" (John 10:30). Unique among all religions, the historical Jesus Christ walked this earth for over thirty years and fulfilled over 250 prophesies made about him by a score of Old Testament prophets living and writing over the preceding fifteen hundred years. His own graphic prophecy of the horrible destruction of Jerusalem and its temple (Matt. 24, Luke 21, and Mark 13), that occurred just as he predicted forty years after his death and resurrection, could stand alone as irrefutable proof of his divinity. All who are truly born again acknowledge, as did Peter, his disciple, and Martha, his friend: "You are the Christ, the son of the living God" (Matt. 16:16 and John 11:27). When the Son of the Living God speaks, his words are not mere theory but fact, and it behooves all mankind to listen: "...my word that goes out from my mouth ...will accomplish what I desire and achieve the purpose for which I sent it" (Isa. 55:11).

This brief witness to Christ focuses uniquely on just six statements Jesus uttered that can profoundly affect anyone regardless of race, religion or lack thereof. The subject of all six sentences consists of two simple monosyllable words that are beyond argument in their clarity. Some parts of God's Word are not easy for the human mind to grasp, but the subject of these six sentences is not among them. The subject of these unshakable certainties is "No one." No one argues about what the phrase, "No one" means. "No one" means not one ... none ... zero. It does not mean some. It does not mean a few. It means none, with no qualifiers, no exceptions, no divine loopholes.

These six factual statements are absolute truth, not relative truth, not true-today-because-I-feel-that-way-but-who-can-say-about-tomorrow. Absolute truth is an out-of-favor term among many today. In their blindness to things of God they refuse to believe that anything could be true yesterday, true today, true tomorrow, true in all circumstances everywhere and forever. That malady is called post-modernism. Sadly, the epidemic has spread even to those who profess to be believers. In a George Barna poll taken shortly after September 11, 2001, 68 percent of those who called themselves born again Christians did not believe in the existence of absolute moral truth. Something is alarmingly wrong here. A Christian by definition believes in the absolute moral truth of God's word proclaimed in the Bible. Sadly, man is a master of self-delusion. He can hold mutually exclusive beliefs without a clue as to the peril of his position.

Jesus has a warning for these poor souls.

> *"Not everyone who says to me, 'Lord, Lord,' will enter the kingdom of heaven, but only he who does the will of my Father who is in heaven. Many will say to me on that day, 'Lord, Lord, did we not prophesy in your name, and in your name drive out demons and perform many miracles?' Then I will tell them plainly, 'I never knew you. Away from me, you evildoers'"(Matt. 7:21-23)!*

Holy Writ makes the concept of absolute truth crystal clear for those who have eyes to see and the most basic understanding of language. Thirty times in the King James Version of the gospels Jesus is quoted beginning a sentence with "Verily." That means "truly." A third of those thirty quotes he repeats, "Verily, verily," for emphasis. He said, "...my words will never pass away" (Matt. 24:35). He said, "I am ... the truth" (John 14:6a). Coming directly from the Son of God's own mouth, that is as absolute as truth can get. The following unshakable certainties are absolute truth from the Son of God.

1
The First Unshakable Certainty

*No one can see the kingdom of God unless
he is born again (John. 3:3b).*

Something must happen before we can see the
things of God and it is not a small thing. It is utterly
decisive! Nothing short of a miraculous rebirth will
give us the sight and insight we need to see God's
truth. Since the fall of Adam and Eve every man,
woman and child has been unable by his or her
own efforts to know God and is not even interested
in looking for him (Romans 3:11). Until God does
something big!

Jesus spoke the words recorded in John 3:3
during a private evening meeting with Nicodemus,
a member of the ruling council of Israel. Sanhedrin
membership was a position of great authority in first
century Israel. It required a superior knowledge of
the Law and the Prophets, what Christians today
call the Old Testament. Nicodemus had seen Jesus
perform some of his miracles and was determined
to meet the man and learn more about him, yet
apparently did not have the nerve to do so in
public. When he found him he asked respectfully,

"Rabbi, we know you are a teacher who has come from God. For no one could perform the miraculous signs you are doing if God were not with him."

Jesus replied, "I tell you the truth, no one can see the kingdom of God unless he is born again" (John 3:3).

Nicodemus would have been familiar with the traumatic, life-changing religious experiences of Moses meeting God in the burning bush (Exod. 3:2) and Isaiah's vision of God on his throne (Isa. 6:1-8), but he did not connect those momentous, life-changing events with what Jesus was saying. He was clueless but curious and his curiosity overcame his fear of appearing ignorant. He asked, "How can a man be born when he is old? ...Surely he cannot enter a second time into his mother's womb to be born" (John 3:4)!

Jesus responded, "...no one can enter the kingdom of God unless he is born of water and the Spirit" (John 3:5).

By this he meant a spiritual rebirth. If we use the classic approach to interpretation of God's Word we let scripture interpret scripture. The cross reference for this passage in my Bible sends me to Titus 3:5, where the Apostle Paul says, "He saved us through the washing of rebirth and renewal by the Holy Spirit." In short, it is a spiritual rebirth, also known as regeneration of the heart, initiated by the Holy Spirit.

God said through the prophet Ezekiel, "I will give you a new heart and put a new spirit in you; I will remove from you your heart of stone and give you a heart of flesh" (Ezek. 36:26).

The result of this spiritual rebirth is a radical change of character, to include seeing the world in a new way. We are given a worldview like God's worldview, only varying in degree of understanding by a factor of one to infinity. We see things we did not see before, including the kingdom of God. We begin to see our sin as an awful insult to a Holy God – a radical change indeed.

God has blessed this unworthy sinner with a spiritual rebirth. I have unbelieving friends and a few family members who cannot for the life of them see what to me is as obvious as the nose on their faces when it comes to things of God. I wonder how they can be so blind (until I remember John 3:3) and they wonder why a reasonably bright guy like me can be so out-to-lunch about how the world works. When we hike the trails of this magnificent Blue Ridge wilderness cathedral at Ridge Haven where I live and work, they see trees and bushes and birds and blue sky and mountains. I see the most spectacular artwork by the infinitely creative hand of the Lord God Almighty. Friends from my fighter pilot days in Vietnam readily agree the supremely self-confident young throttle jockey they knew back then has undergone a radical change. In fact, a commanding officer that I had not seen in three decades, who had mellowed in his old age, politely observed, "I do not recall your being so much into spiritual things back then." I am grateful to God he could see a difference.

But there is another critical, blockbuster revelation in Jesus' straightforward words to Nicodemus that few Christians understand. The majority view in Christianity today is that "coming to faith" entails a conscious decision after a careful examination of God's promises. They proclaim that a "seeker," of his own free will, can chose to believe, confess he has been sinful, ask God's forgiveness, and be born again. That decision to repent and believe is their good work, which, when combined with God's gracious offer, leads to spiritual rebirth. But wait a minute. No one can examine what he cannot see, let alone make a decision about it. Jesus said, "No one can see the kingdom of God unless he is born again." He was saying that the miraculous change, the spiritual rebirth that opens ones eyes to see the things of God, must happen first. In words as clear and concise as words can be, he is saying our rebirth, the regeneration of our heart, the radical change in our character, must precede our seeing. It is what makes the seeing possible. And it is an exclusive work of God from start to finish. God and God alone initiates and implements our rebirth, and we have no more control over it than we had over our physical birth. The Apostle Paul put it aptly:

"But because of his great love for us, God, who is rich in mercy, made us alive with Christ even when we were dead in transgressions – it is by grace you have been saved" (Eph. 2:4-5).

Dead people cannot see the kingdom of God. Dead people cannot make choices or decisions. Man is spiritually dead in his sin (transgressions) until God in his mercy makes him alive in Christ. We can take no credit for our spiritual rebirth whatsoever – a humbling experience, as Moses and Isaiah learned. The first miracle in the series of miracles that leads to the unshakable certainty of salvation for saved sinners is a work of God alone. There is a wonderful word for that. It is grace – God's unmerited favor.

Without that act of grace we see nothing of God's truth, we seek nothing of God. The Apostle Paul had a "no one" of his own in support of this. He said in Romans 3:11, "There is... no one who seeks God." In Ephesians 2:8-9 he also gives us a reason for why God did it that way: "It is by grace you have been saved...so that no one can boast." That is, no one can boast he did it on his own, or even helped.

If you are as engrossed in this as I hope you are, you must be asking yourself, as Nicodemus was, how, if God initiates spiritual rebirth, does he decide on whom to shower such amazing grace. Jesus, knowing the mind of Nicodemus, had an answer for that too. He said, in effect, that is not for you to know – only God knows that. His actual words were,

> *You should not be surprised at my saying, "You must be born again." The wind blows wherever it pleases. You hear its sound, but you cannot tell where it comes from or where it is going. So it is with everyone born of the Spirit (John 3:7-8).*

As a scholar in the Law and the Prophets, Nicodemus should not have had any quarrel with the first sentence. He should have been able to discern from the history of his people that incorrigible Israel, to a man, was desperately in need of a divine makeover. Even the Old Testament heroes had feet of clay. Abraham was too impatient to wait on the Lord and fathered a son by his wife's servant girl. Moses was a murderer and Jacob was a rascal who stiffed his brother over and over again. The great King David was an adulterer and murderer. Repeatedly Israel had broken the Ten Commandments and been punished severely by God.

But it is the last sentence that really blew Nicodemus away. Jesus said, "The wind blows wherever it pleases. ...[Y]ou cannot tell where it comes from or where it is going. So it is with everyone born of the Spirit" (John 3:8).

In other words, an infinitely wise God works according to holy parameters unknown to man in choosing which hearts he will mercifully regenerate. Amazing grace! Just as no one knows where the wind came from or where it is going, likewise no one knows whom God has chosen to bless with spiritual rebirth.

This was not a new revelation. As early as the second book of the Bible God told Moses: "I will have mercy on whom I will have mercy" (Exod. 33:19).

But apparently the Pharisees had not thought through this revelation to its logical conclusion. The Apostle Paul quoted Exodus 33:19 and then expounded on this vital truth in his letter to the Romans. He said, "It does not, therefore, depend on man's desire or effort, but on God's mercy" (Romans 9:16).

Nicodemus was at the limits of his mental capacity. "How can this be?" he asked. Like millions of people today, casual Christians and unbelievers alike, Nicodemus was oblivious to God's absolute lordship over his creation. God's continuous activity to preserve and govern his creation was a fact beyond Nicodemus' understanding. Such divine controlling activity is called by another wonderful word – providence. C. H. Spurgeon, an eloquent preacher of nineteenth century London, said that "every particle of dust that dances in the sunbeam moves not one molecule more nor less than God wills." Jesus said, "...even the very hairs of your head are all numbered" (Matt 10:30, Luke 12:7). That is micromanagement to the infinite degree. That is providence. It is a resounding refutation of that preposterous theory, elevated to the status of a religion in some of our culture's loftiest towers of academe, that the universe is governed by chance.

Jesus did not let up or give up on Nicodemus. He said, "You are Israel's teacher ... and do you not understand these things?" (John 3:10).

Surely this man was humiliated by these words. The Sanhedrin was the highest church authority in the land and it was probably the first time Nicodemus' authority and knowledge had ever been so thoroughly refuted, and by a tradesman's son from the boondocks.

Then Jesus did a gracious thing. He explained to Nicodemus the kind of mercy all Israel was talking about. He told him, face-to-face, up close in a personal audience, precisely what was required of him to achieve eternal life. As a Pharisee, Nicodemus would have believed in eternal life and it would have been something he would have wanted with all his heart and soul. Surely it was a major part of his motivation when he decided to search out Jesus in the evening.

Jesus told him the way to eternal life. "For God so loved the world, that he gave his only begotten Son, that whosoever believeth in him should not perish, but have everlasting life" (John 3:16 KJV).

While that quote is common knowledge today, whether or not it is believed, every phrase of this sentence must have boggled the mind of Nicodemus. Jews proudly believed that they alone were God's chosen people and they despised the rest of the world. Yet here was Jesus saying that God loved the whole world. We also know from Jewish law that God having a son would have been an incomprehensible concept to any Jew. And Jesus was saying God loved the world immensely, so much he was willing to "give" his only son. At this point in time Nicodemus did not know half the cost of that "giving." To promise eternal life for no more than the price of belief that Jesus was the Son of God would have been absurd to a Pharisee, as it is to many unbelievers today. Most Pharisees were so practiced at public displays of piety that they could have easily faked belief, as if God could be fooled as readily as their fellow Jews. They spent nearly all their waking moments trying to earn their way to heaven by works they considered good. Nicodemus did not understand that he could not in a hundred lifetimes do enough good works to earn his way into the infinite holiness of heaven. Yet here was a man professing to be the Son of God, right in his face in the quiet of a private home, telling a sincere inquirer in words so simple yet so overwhelming, how easily he might have eternal life. If God had chosen to regenerate the heart of Nicodemus first, these words would have sent him dancing into the night. He would have gone skipping through the marble-paved streets of nighttime Jerusalem shouting the gospel at the top of his lungs. "GOOD NEWS! GOOD NEWS! For God so loved the world, that he gave his only begotten Son, that whosoever believeth in him should not perish, but have everlasting life!"

Renowned Scottish preacher and editor, Maurice Roberts, had this to say about "whosoever believeth in him." It was one of those brilliantly phrased questions like Jesus used that answered itself. To ask the question was to know the answer. Roberts quoted John 3:16, concluding with, "...whosoever believeth in him should not perish, but have everlasting life!" Then he said, "Whosoever will may come, and whosoever will may ask and receive Christ, heaven and glory. But have you asked? And if you have, who made you to differ from those who did not?"

It added one thousand watts of light to a truth I thought I already knew pretty well. I believe in Jesus because, and only because, God regenerated my heart and opened my eyes to his truth. I wrote Pastor Roberts' words in the margin of my Bible in April 1992 and memorized them. Now, when I see a John 3:16 bumper sticker or sign at a football game, Jesus' promise comes to mind along with Pastor Roberts' self-answering questions. I find unshakable certainty in them.

God's Word does not tell us what became of Nicodemus, but this much we do know. From the text it appears he left the meeting with Jesus with his unchanged heart broken, shaking his head in utter bewilderment as he walked down the street. At some point after talking to Jesus, though, Nicodemus must have experienced spiritual rebirth, perhaps as he witnessed his crucifixion and recalled his words. John 19:38 says he helped Joseph of Arimathea take the body of Jesus from the cross and prepare and bury it. Both men were Sanhedrin members and would have been at great risk in doing this. It is reasonable to assume that their belief that Jesus was who he said he was gave them the courage to do it. We also know that after the great outpouring of the Holy Spirit at Pentecost, the powerful preaching of Peter and the other disciples in the months and years that followed in Jerusalem led to a "large number of [Jewish] priests" (Acts 6:7) being counted among the born-again in Jerusalem. The rest of the New Testament reveals that the word "believe," as used by Jesus, entails much more that just intellectual assent to his existence. It includes heart knowledge as well as head knowledge and not least it includes obedience. If you truly believe Jesus is who he said he is, then you will obey his commands, and because of your spiritual rebirth, you will do so heartily.

No one can see the kingdom of God unless he is born again (John 3:3).

It is an unshakable certainty in an uncertain world. It is the first miracle in the divine order of salvation. Can you see the kingdom of God in your mind's eye? If you can, thank God for regenerating your heart. If you cannot, why not ask the Lord God Almighty for spiritual rebirth? The story of your life has already been written and is on file at the highest levels of authority. Perhaps the next chapter of your biography begins with your prayer for a regenerated heart.

2

The Second Unshakable Certainty

No one can come to me unless the Father who sent me draws him (John 6:44a).

God does not regenerate our hearts and turn us loose on our own to repent of our sins, trust in Jesus, obey him and find our way to heaven as best we can. Having initiated and completed the miracle of our spiritual rebirth (Chapter 1), Jesus goes on to explain that God has much work yet to do on our behalf. We can see the kingdom of God, we can read and ponder the promises of Christ in the Bible, but we cannot come to Christ, we cannot believe his reality, incorrigible kids that we are, unless God the Father takes the initiative once again. Jesus said, "No one can come to me unless the Father who sent me draws him" (John 6:44a).

Whether we are cold, lukewarm or on fire for the kingdom of God, we are at the bottom of the well and powerless to ascend to the smiling countenance of Christ looking down on us from that circle of daylight at the wellhead. Just like our spiritual rebirth, nothing happens unless our gracious God acts. And again he does. God has begun a work in us, and only he knows the timing of each step, but he never quits mid-project. His plan leaves nothing to chance, including the actions of a capricious sinner.

God the Father draws us to the Son. There are those who argue the Greek word here translated "draws," means "to entice." These are the same folks who want to believe that coming to faith is at least partially, if not completely, our accomplishment. They say God puts the offer on the table and man either accepts it or rejects it. But that is not what Jesus is saying in the first two unshakable certainties about "No one." He is saying, no one can see the kingdom of God unless he is spiritually reborn, and having seen it, no one can come to Christ our Savior unless God draws him (like a pail of water from a well), neither of which we have any control over whatsoever. The only way we can get from the bottom of that sinful well where we have been frolicking, oblivious to our dire straits, is for God to act. First he opens our eyes to our dilemma, and then he lowers the bucket on a rope down to us and draws us up. Like the water, we are non-participating passengers in the bucket. At that point we may not even be too crazy about leaving our cool well. Water from a well can end up in the digestive system of an ox, and how much fun would that be? God's plan for us might include an unpleasant sojourn, in, say, the belly of a whale (Jonah 1:17), or some other seemingly unappealing place. Such thoughts are nearly always present, prior to and even after commitment, as one considers the kingdom of God and the implications of obedience to him.

Just like the water in the bucket, as we are being drawn up we are helpless to climb out and jump back into the well. We are under the total control of the one cranking the pulley that inexorably lifts us to a higher plane, into the bright Light of the World. Again using scripture to interpret scripture, the Greek word here translated "draw," appears in only one other place in the Bible, in Acts 16:19, and it is translated "dragged." The Apostle Paul had just cast a demon out of a slave girl who had prophetic powers that her owners used for profit.

When the owners of the slave girl realized that their hope of making money was gone, they seized Paul and Silas and dragged them into the marketplace to face the authorities (Acts 16:19).

It seems abundantly clear that the interpretation is "compel," with or without the cooperation of the person being compelled and that the drawing water metaphor is correct.

Jesus however did not just mention this great unshakable certainty in passing. He was speaking to a large crowd in the lakeside city of Capernaum on the northwest shore of the Sea of Galilee. It was most of the same five thousand folks he miraculously fed the day before on the other side of the lake by multiplying a boy's five small loaves of bread and two small fish. The crowd was thinking he was the Messiah all Israel had been expecting for centuries. In their blindness they, as almost all Jews, interpreted the Old Testament prophecies of a Messiah coming to mean he would be an earthly king who would free them from the cruel bondage to Rome and rule like kings David and Solomon of old. They wanted to force him to be their king. Jesus knew that was on their minds and he had

35

given them the slip the day before. When they finally caught up with him again in Capernaum, Jesus accused them of wanting another free meal. Then he told them to work not for food that spoils but for food that endures to eternal life, which he, "the Son of Man" (his favorite name for himself), would give them. They asked, "What must we do to do the works God requires?" Just like Nicodemus and all Israel, they were oriented to works and ritual. For example, the sacrificial system down at the magnificent Temple in Jerusalem was a major part of the culture and the economy. Animals were sacrificed every day. Rivers of blood flowed down through the alter gutters and torrents of money flowed into the Temple.

Jesus' reply was a rephrased version of what he told Nicodemus in private and what he preached in public all over Judea and Galilee. "The work of God is this: to believe in the one he has sent" (John 6:29).

They knew by this time that he was claiming to be the one sent by God. Yet the crowd still had the nerve to demand another miracle, "that we may see and believe you" (John 6:30).

Jesus ignored the question and proceeded to explain to them what he meant by the "food that endures to eternal life." He said,

I am the bread of life. He who comes to me will never go hungry, and he who believes in me will never be thirsty. But as I told you, you have seen me and still you do not believe. All that the Father gives me will come to me, and whoever comes to me I will never drive away (John 6:35-37).

Clearly they did not get his metaphorical illustrations and Jesus told them he knew they did not get it and he explained why in the last sentence. They had not believed and come to him because they were not on the Father's secret sacred list of those he planned to mercifully regenerate and draw to his Son – or perhaps it was not yet their appointed time for spiritual rebirth. These words are profoundly comforting to the born again, but utter mumbo-jumbo to those unregenerate ears that cannot hear and eyes that cannot see God's truth. Too bad. Way too bad indeed, because Jesus' next words are a profound and wonderful revelation.

> *For I have come down from heaven not to do my will but to do the will of him who sent me. And this is the will of him who sent me, that I shall lose none of all that he has given me, but raise them up at the last day. For my Father's will is that everyone who looks to the Son and believes in him shall have eternal life, and I will raise him up at the last day (John 6:38-40).*

Repetition is the mark of a good teacher and the most often used grammatical device for emphasis in the Bible. Jesus repeats what he has said before and builds on it, then repeats it again. Those God the Father has planned to bless with spiritual rebirth will be given ("drawn") to his Son and the Son will never drive them away and will lose none of them. "None" and "never" are in the same class with "no one." They allow no exceptions. They are absolutes. When spoken by Jesus they are divine guarantees with the highest quality collateral.

Then twice in two sentences Jesus says that he will raise them up at the end of history. They would have understood "raise them up," a Jewish colloquialism for the dead rising from the grave to life again, but they were hung up on his claim to have come from heaven. They knew his legal earthly father, Joseph the carpenter from Nazareth, and they knew his grandparents.

"How can he say he came from heaven?" they asked (John 6:42). With our great blessing of hindsight – we have read the rest of the Bible – perhaps we should cut these poor lost souls some slack here. After all, while some traditions hold otherwise, the Bible mentions only one virgin – Mary – who gave birth to a child conceived by the Holy Spirit, a miracle indeed.

Jesus told them to knock off the grumbling and summarized all that he had told them in one potent sentence, one unshakable certainty: "No one can come to me unless the Father who sent me draws him, and I will raise him up at the last day." He backed it up with a quotation from Isaiah 54:13: "It is written in the Prophets: 'They will all be taught by God.' Everyone who listens to the Father and learns from him comes to me" (John 6:45). Debate was a popular form of social intercourse in first century Israel, and quoting from the Law and the Prophets to prove a point was the heavy artillery.

Jesus then repeated his "I am the bread of life" metaphor and expounded on it at length yet again, but he was losing his audience. They thought he was talking literally, explaining some kind of bizarre cannibalistic ritual. Even his disciples found it a difficult statement. Jesus had not yet instituted the Lord's Supper, which would clear up these comments for them. But in the pagan world over a century later the Romans still thought Christianity, or "The Way" as it was known then, was a cannibalistic religion.

We cannot know the infinite mind of God, but Jesus' tone, alone with his disciples after this mass rejection by the people, has a hint of sadness. "Does this offend you [too]?" (John 6:61b).

With infinite patience the Son of God, emptied of every heavenly glory except love, that he might live as the incarnate Son of Man for a time, began again to explain to his beloved disciples.

> *"The Spirit gives life; the flesh counts for nothing. The words I have spoken to you are spirit and they are life. Yet there are some of you who do not believe."* *For Jesus had known from the beginning which of them did not believe and who would betray him. He went on to say, "This is why I told you that no one can come to me unless the Father has enabled him"* *(John 6:63-65).*

There it is again, the second unshakable certainty repeated and rephrased to say "enabled" instead of "draws." My computer's thesaurus pulls up "empowered, confirmed, authorized," when I type in "enabled." While drawing a pail of water illustrates a critical aspect of who is in charge when God "draws" us, "enabled" points up another. I mentioned in the last chapter that some folks think they come to God of their own "free will." Now that is an inflammatory phrase in some denominational circles, and we are going to cautiously venture into deep theological waters because it is important. Martin Luther, a bright, courageous icon of the faith wrote a whole book about free will entitled, *Bondage of the Will*. Two hundred years later Jonathan Edwards, a heavyweight Puritan theologian credited with preaching the greatest sermon ever preached on the North American continent, wrote a book entitled, *The Freedom of the Will*. In spite of titles that implied they were arguing opposite sides of the issue, both reached the same conclusion. We are indeed free to choose in God's world, to make decisions based on our perceptions of the facts at hand combined and tempered with varying degrees of our wants and desires. Our amazing Creator, who wrote the story of our life before we were born, so orders our wants and desires and perceptions and understanding so as to control our lives according to his script without violating our free will. In the words of R. C. Sproul, he "inclines our will." Paul told the Philippians, "...for it is God who works in you to will and to act according to his good purpose" (Phil. 2:13). Or, as Jesus said, he "enables" us to do what he wants because it is what we want to do. (See also Dan. 1:9, Ezra 1:1, and Exod. 12:36.) As Maurice Roberts said, "Who made you to differ from those who did not [ask]?" Amazing grace!

But alas for Jesus' audience that day, scripture says "many of his disciples" left and "walked with him no more" (John 6:66). Men who had sat in rapt attention at his knee, who had dined with him, witnessed his miracles up close, listened to hours of his teaching, rejected him. Can there be a more tragic event than to see and hear God in the flesh ... and reject him?

The twelve however were still there and Jesus asked them, "You do not want to leave too, do you?" (John 6:67).

It must have been a low point for the disciples to see so many people witness such a great miracle of feeding and reject Jesus. Just the night before the disciples, with fear and trembling, had also witnessed him walking on storm-tossed water. But even they were bewildered. Even impetuous Peter sounded shaken. He did not say, "No problem, Lord. We understood it perfectly." He said, "Lord, to whom shall we go? You have the words of eternal life. We believe and know that you are the Holy One of God" (John 6:68).

Dear reader, do you find the Son of God's unshakable certainties hard sayings? Are you offended that Almighty God chooses to show mercy to some among the sinners of every tribe and nation of the world, and he regenerates them for eternal life for reasons we may never know? Will you reject the Savior and eternal life because no matter how self-sufficient you may think you are, you are powerless to believe in Jesus Christ unless God miraculously opens your eyes to his truth and then draws you to His Son? Or, enabled by God, will you ask him to change your heart and draw near to him, knowing, like Peter, that he has the words of life, that he is who he said he is, "the Bread of Life," whether or not your feeble mind grasps every nuance of every truth? If so, you will know, as the hymn writer knew who set these poetic truths to a George Chadwick melody:

> *I sought the Lord and afterward I knew*
> *He moved my soul to seek him, seeking me;*
> *It was not I that found, O Savior true;*
> *No, I was found of thee.*[1]

He was inspired to write that hymn from the text of 1 John 4:19, where Jesus' favorite disciple said, "We love because he first loved us." That reality is the most important lesson you'll ever learn in your life.

> *No one can see the kingdom of God*
> *unless he is born again.*

"No one..."

> *No one can come to me unless the*
> *Father who sent me draws him.*
> *(John 3:3; 6:44)*

These are unshakable certainties in an uncertain world.

ENDNOTES

---

1. Anonymous, I Sought the Lord and Afterward I Knew

3

The Third Unshakable Certainty

I am the way and the truth and the life. No one comes to the Father except through me. (John 14:6)

Nothing gets a Christian in more trouble more quickly with postmodern unbelievers in our culture than this third unshakable certainty. To profess a belief in one exclusive way to heaven is to be branded intolerant. There are dozens, maybe hundreds of pathways to heaven professed in religiously diverse nations today, and the postmodern standard is to celebrate them all, quaint little cultural customs that they are. Whatever gets you through the night. After all, the postmodernists say, there is no such thing as right and wrong or good and evil and absolute truth. If it works for you and does not hurt me then we are all happy. Anything goes, any destiny, any way as long as you do not claim your worldview is the only way. Well, the Bible proclaims there is only one way, as we see from these "no one" statements we are studying, making Christians "dangerous fundamentalists" in our culture, a totally incorrect characterization that has found its way onto the printed page in a number of major periodicals.

None of this godless rant sends the slightest tremor through the unshakable certainty declared by the Son of God. In the Olivet Discourse Jesus declared, "Heaven and earth will pass away, but my words will never pass away" (Matt. 24:35, Mark 13:31, Luke 21:33). Two thousand years after he spoke these words to twelve ordinary tradesmen in an olive grove overlooking a small middle-eastern city, his words can still be found in the all-time best-selling book – the Bible – and on the lips of millions of people. His words have withstood far worse assault than name-calling. The effort to remove God's words from public places by various liberal political and legal groups is but a minor irritant compared to the crucifixions, stonings, and gruesome arena carnage of Rome that the early church endured. Not only did they endure the tribulation that slaughtered thousands, but they thrived. Today a magazine called *Voice of the Martyrs* reports of the slaughter of Christians in Asia and Africa. It appears that where adversity is the worst, God's church grows the fastest. Like Jesus and Stephen with their dying breath, we should be asking God to have mercy on these desperately lost souls who know not what they are doing. But for the amazing grace that gives Christians a miraculous spiritual rebirth, we would all be marching in their ranks into the fiery abyss.

"I am the way and the truth and the life. No one comes to the Father except through me" (John 14:6). Jesus spoke these words of supreme comfort to his disciples, and us, at the Last Supper in the upper room, during what had been a traumatic week of Passover that was about to get much worse. Jerusalem was a roiling sea of Jewish humanity chafing under brutally oppressive Roman rule during Passover Week, with hundreds of thousands flooding the city ready to fulfill their required sacrifices at the Temple. Jesus had arrived a few days earlier to cheering multitudes shouting "Hosanna," which means literally, "Save us now." After three years of missionary work his reputation for miracle making, if not his message, was known throughout Israel. The Roman Procurator, Pontius Pilate, knew what the Jewish Messiah wish was all about and in order to crush any possible revolt had brought military reinforcements into Fortress Antonia. It rose above the northwest corner of the Temple compound, guarding the courtyard with sentinels carefully watching the crowd of Jewish pilgrims preparing to worship. On crowded streets throughout the city soldiers were posted, watching for the first sign of trouble that could so quickly turn to bloody rioting, as it had often before.

Two days earlier Jesus had told his disciples in graphic terms of the pending fiery destruction of the temple and virtual leveling of the holy city of Jerusalem (Matt. 24, Luke 21, Mark 13). He had also warned them that many of them in their missionary travels would die awful deaths, just as he would this very Passover. Earlier in the week he had stirred up a terrible fuss by driving the moneychangers out of the crowded Temple compound with a whip. They all knew the Sanhedrin wanted him dead. When he told them he was going to die, the disciples still did not understand it.

At their Passover Meal Jesus instituted a new memorial service, a formal act of worship that came to be called the Lord's Supper. He explained to them that eating bread and drinking wine in remembrance of him should be done periodically until he came again. The broken bread and the wine were to be powerful symbolic reminders of Jesus' broken body and shed blood on the cross, which they still did not understand, but would shortly as the agony for Jesus was only hours away. This new Lord's Supper was a solemn occasion. Its deep significance dawned on them in the first one celebrated after the death of Jesus and ascension to heaven. So it remains to this day, a holy sacrament instituted by Jesus himself.

Then Jesus accused one of them of being a traitor, but in words only he and the traitor understood. Judas beat a hasty retreat from the room, leaving everyone else totally confused as to what was happening. The tension was palpable in that quiet, secluded upper room as Jesus began to preach his own funeral sermon. "Do not let your hearts be troubled. Trust in God; trust also in me. In my Father's house are many rooms; if it were not so, I would have told you. I am going there to prepare a place for you" (John 14:1-2).

These were soothing words to his disciples, conveying a sense of sublime peace to them and to millions of grieving Christians at millions of funerals in the two millennia since. He continued, "And if I go and prepare a place for you, I will come back and take you to be with me that you also may be where I am. You know the way to the place where I am going" (John 14:3-4).

Then anguished Thomas broke in, with no apology for interrupting his Teacher, "Lord, we don't know where you are going, so how can we know the way?"

Ever-patient Jesus, who knew Thomas' heart far better than he knew it himself, answered, "I am the way and the truth and the life. No one comes to the Father except through me" (John 14:6).

God the Father is the glorious end, and God the Son is the only way. There is no other way. The life of which Jesus speaks is not mere existence but fulfillment both now and forever according to God's design for us. Believe that and you have done all that God requires. By Christ's atonement – his death on the cross as a substitute for those God has chosen to be saved – we are justified, that is we are made acceptable to a Holy God. The demands of his law have been fulfilled in the righteousness of his Son (Romans 3:24).

As Paul told the Corinthians, "All this is from God, who reconciled us to himself through Christ" (2 Cor. 5:18).

There are a great many people professing to be Christians today who think there will be a balance scale in the throne-room of God on Judgment Day, and if the good deeds outweigh the bad, they have won eternal life. That is also the Islamic view of Judgment Day, but it is not biblical. Such a scale is not at the heart of Christianity. The cross of Christ is at the heart of Christianity, and the grace by which Christ's atonement covers his people. This is one of the unique features of Christianity among all the world's religions. It is our belief, our faith in Christ as our Savior, that God wants to know on Judgment Day, not our woefully inadequate accomplishments, and he can read the heart. Do not meet your maker with a resume of your good works. The best you have done is as filthy rags in the presence of an infinitely Holy God (Isa. 64:6).

Paul comes through again: "For it is by grace you have been saved, through faith – and this not from yourselves, it is the gift of God – not by works, so that no one can boast" (Eph. 2:8-9).

An old friend I had not seen in many years found his way to my mountain community a while back. At breakfast on a Sunday morning we invited him to go to church with us. He politely declined with the puniest of excuses but then went to some pains to tell us that he was a "good enough Christian to get into heaven," as if God graded our works and he did so on a curve. His brilliant mind was closed to any other way of looking at it. May God yet regenerate his heart.

On Judgment Day you will probably be too traumatized to speak. You may even find yourself face down before the throne. Claim the Son in your heart and God will know.

A mature, eloquent, Holy Spirit-filled Peter would say a few years later, building on Jesus' "no one" certainties: "Salvation is found in no one else, for there is no other name under heaven given to men by which we must be saved" (Acts 4:12).

My little sister asked her priest once, "Is Jesus the only way to heaven?" He replied, oh so politically correctly, "He's one way."

She got bad advice. When she asked me for confirmation I quoted John 14:6 to her and rested my case. This unshakable certainty does not require a Bible scholar to explain. It can stand alone in any audience. May it stand prominently in your heart and at the center of your mind every waking moment of your life – an eternal reality.

No one can see the kingdom of God
unless he is born again.

*No one can come to me unless
the Father who sent me draws him.
No one comes to the Father
except through me.
(John 3:3; 6:44; 14:6)*

These are unshakable certainties in an uncertain world.

4

The Fourth Unshakable Certainty

No one takes it [life] from me, but I lay it down of my own accord. I have authority to lay it down and authority to take it up again.
(John 10:18a)

First Jesus was flogged with a three-strand leather whip with pieces of sharp bone woven into the ends. The typical Jewish flogging was "forty stripes less one," or thirteen strokes with a three-strand whip, but the Roman floggings were usually worse. The victim was stripped and bent over a stump about three feet tall and tied there. The lashes were applied diagonally from the front of the victim so that the stripes ran from the right shoulder diagonally down across the back and around the waist and between the legs, and then likewise diagonally from the left shoulder. When it was over the damage looked less like stripes than raw hamburger. Sometimes it was fatal.

Then they jammed a crown of thorns on his head, sending rivulets of blood down his cheeks and neck. A massive timber, the crossbeam to his cross, was set across his shoulders. His arms were extended and tied to it. A detail of Roman soldiers led Jesus and two other condemned men through the streets of Jerusalem, mobbed with pilgrims in town for Passover. It was less than a mile from Pontius Pilate's palace out through the city gate to Golgotha on the northwest side of town. Jesus nearly died en route.

Death by crucifixion was the most horrifying, most agonizing and slowest public death the mind of man could conceive in that era, and Golgotha was a very visible spot. It was a high, skull-shaped hill near two main arteries into the city, and there, in view of many thousands of Jewish pilgrims, our Savior suffered the wrath of God the Father for the sins of those he loved.

With a series of extraordinary supernatural signs seen neither before nor since, God made it plain to every living soul in the vicinity of Israel that this was the major event of the ages. At noon, after Jesus had been hanging in inconceivable pain for two or three hours, the sky became dark as midnight and it was not an eclipse of the sun. For three hours it was pitch black. The earth quaked, boulders split open, tombstones rolled away from tomb entrances and "many holy people who had died were raised to life...and appeared to many people" (Matt. 27:52-3). Between three and four in the afternoon Jesus said in a loud voice, "It is finished" (John 19:30) and he died. The centurion in charge of the crucifixion detail, who had witnessed it all, said, "Surely this man was the Son of God" (Mark 15:39).

Jesus died right at the time that thousands of lambs' throats were being cut before the altar in front of the Temple for the Passover sacrifice. The real sacrificial lamb, the Lamb of God, as John the Baptist called him (John 1:29, 36), the one that fourteen centuries of unblemished one-year-old male lambs had been symbolizing and pointing to, died, once, for all his people. At that same moment the curtain within the great temple that separated the Holy Place from the Most Holy Place "was torn in two from top to bottom" (Matt 27:51). That curtain was thirty feet high and thirty feet wide and a handbreadth thick. The Most Holy Place, the home of the Ark of the Covenant before it disappeared in the destruction of Solomon's Temple five centuries earlier, was where the spirit of God symbolically resided. Only the High Priest was allowed in that room and then only once a year. By the miracle of the torn curtain God was telling his people that now, through the shed blood of Jesus Christ, all who believe could draw near to God.

The prosecution and execution of Jesus Christ was a singular travesty of human justice. Jewish law pertaining to capital punishment was more exhaustive in due process and protective of human rights than the modern American legal system. If there had been a court of appeal above the Sanhedrin in first century Israel, Jesus' case would have been tossed out on a dozen major procedural points, to say nothing of a lack of evidence, and Jesus' prosecutors would have been prosecuted themselves for perjury. To accuse one unjustly of a capital offense was a crime punishable by death in Jewish law.

But even at that Jesus' crucifixion was not a disastrous defeat. His was not an extraordinary ministry cut short by catastrophe. It happened precisely as it was planned in the throne room of

God. Jesus indicated as much in an exchange with Pontius Pilate at his trial:

> *Pilate said, "Don't you realize I have power either to free you or to crucify you?"*
>
> *Jesus answered, "You would have no power over me if it were not given to you from above"*
> *(John 19: 10-11).*

As God inclines the will of those who have been spiritually reborn so as not to violate their free will while accomplishing his purposes, likewise he uses the acts of evil men for his purposes too. Pilate would have had no power over Jesus were it not part of God's plan (Exod. 9:16, Romans 9:17).

All men are sinners since the fall of Adam. I have unchurched friends who refuse to believe that, but if it is not self-evident to the most casual observer, the Bible surely makes it crystal clear. Paul told the Romans, "all have sinned and fall short of the glory of God" (Romans 3:23). The writer of Ecclesiastes said, "There is not a righteous man on earth who does what is right and never sins" (Eccles. 7:20). King David prayed in his most moving confessional Psalm, "Surely I was sinful at birth, sinful from the time my mother conceived me" (Ps. 51:5). These statements leave no room for misunderstanding and are too powerful to ignore.

When I covet that big house with the fabulous view my friend owns further up the mountain (breaking the Tenth Commandment – Exod. 20:17), I am as guilty of sin as any murderer (the Sixth Commandment – Exod. 20:13). When I feel self-satisfied at my own "wordsmithing" I put myself ahead of God who gave me the gift and I break the First Commandment ("You shall have no other gods before me." – Exod. 20:3). Even thoughts of sinning are sinning. If God were to merely over-look all our "little sins," like "white lies," he would not meet his own standard of perfect justice. The fact remains, no one is worthy of a relationship with an infinitely Holy God, and we are as helpless to correct this as we are to be born again.

Paul gets to the heart of it: "all have sinned and fall short of the glory of God" (Rom 3:23).

So, once again, God acts to save his people. Sin must be punished for God's perfect justice to be served. Under the Old Testament law God accepted the death and blood of animals as a substitute for the death the sinner deserved.

> *"He is to lay his hand on the head of the burnt offering, and it will be accepted on his behalf to make atonement for him" (Lev 1:4). ...Then, before the LORD, you will be clean from all your sins (Lev. 16:30b).*

The Old Testament book of Exodus details the elaborate ritual required in the performance of animal sacrifices. The animal had to be a perfect specimen without the smallest blemish, a foreshadowing of the ultimate perfect sacrifice that Jesus became. No one could participate in or even view such a bloody, gruesome ritual without getting a powerful sense that a righteous and Holy God in his infinite wrath hated sin and it was indeed a matter of life or death. Animals were sacrificed every day for over fourteen centuries, but (big but)...

> *The [Old Testament] law [governing animal sacrifice] is only a shadow of the good things that are coming – not the realities themselves. For this reason it can never, by the same sacrifices repeated endlessly year after year, make perfect those who draw near*

to worship ... because it is impossible for the blood of bulls and goats to take away sins (Heb. 10:1, 4).

The only thing that could make sinners perfect in the eyes of God is a perfect atoning sacrifice, and the only thing perfect in the whole universe is God. So God the Father sent his only Son. Jesus Christ, the Son of God and sinless man, was sacrificed once for all those who are chosen for spiritual rebirth and eternal life.

Forty years after Jesus died on the cross, the Temple and all Jerusalem were destroyed, just as he prophesied in the Olivet Discourse (Matt. 24 et al.) because, in Jesus' own words, "you did not recognize the time of God's coming to you" (Luke 19:44), meaning his coming as a man. There is another cosmic reason for the total destruction of Jerusalem besides God's wrath for Israel's moral failures. Today, nearly 2,000 years later, the Temple has never been rebuilt and there are still no Jewish animal sacrifices, and for good providential reasons – none are needed. The crucifixion, the shedding of God the Son's blood, was all that was needed. It was shed on Passover, a Jewish celebration of God's freeing them from the bondage of slavery in Egypt. This precious blood of the Savior freed all believers from the bondage of sin. It was the keystone of God's eternal plan to save his people.

The pain and agony of crucifixion is beyond comprehension. For Jesus to lay down his life in such a way of his own accord demonstrates a love that is beyond human capacity. Jesus said, "Greater love has no one than this, that he lay down his life for his friends. You are my friends if you do what I command" (John 15:13-14).

The "if" in the last sentence is not a qualifier for friendship, but evidence – fruit of the Spirit – of a born again heart, wrought by a gracious God. Jesus is saying there is no greater love than the love he is demonstrating by dying such a terrible death for them, his friends.

As Charles Wesley, the prolific eighteenth century hymn writer, wrote,

> *Amazing love. How can it be,*
> *that thou my God shouldst die for me?*[1]

No one who understands the fearsome wrath of a Holy God, and the terrible consequences of personal sin against him, can help but be thunderstruck by his infinite love for his people and by the gracious gift of his blood as atonement for their sins that guarantees eternal life with him. By the most heroic act the world has ever witnessed, Jesus Christ, the Savior of his people, will escort them to the throne of grace and God's "glorious presence without fault and with great joy" (Jude 24).

On my office wall a Distinguished Flying Cross hangs, awarded to me when I was a brash young combat fighter pilot in Vietnam. Many western nations use a cross in their medals for heroism. The British have the Victoria Cross, Germany has the Iron Cross and France the Croix de guerre for the very reason that it symbolizes the most heroic act in human history – the death of Christ on the cross for his friends. Every day when I see that cross on my wall I am reminded that God in his providence saved my life on a Sunday morning in the summer of 1968 – there is no earthly reason why I am here to tell the story. But greater by far, I am reminded, as I go to work, that the Son of God died there to save my soul.

Do you see a pattern developing here? A plan emerging? It is God's plan of salvation for sinners. Our God leaves nothing to chance. Every step is initiated and controlled by him down to the smallest detail. His merciful providence extends to the microscopic. There is not one aberrant atom anywhere.

> *No one can see the kingdom of God*
> *unless he is born again.*
> *No one can come to me unless the Father*
> *who sent me draws him.*
> *No one comes to the Father except through me.*
> *No one takes it [life] from me, but I lay it down*
> *of my own accord.*
> *(John 3:3; 6:44; 14:6; 10:18a)*

These are unshakable certainties in an uncertain world.

ENDNOTES
_____

1. Charley Wesley, And Can It Be That I Should Gain

5

The Fifth Unshakable Certainty

My sheep listen to my voice... I give them eternal life... no one can snatch them out of my hand (John 10:27-28).

Sheep provide perhaps the most spiritually sumptuous metaphor in the Bible. The word appears 205 times in the Old and New Testaments, and Jesus is quoted using the word thirty-nine times in the gospels as a metaphor in his parables – his illustrations of eternal truths. Sheep ranked right up there with bread among the most important essentials of first century middle-eastern life.

While living in Spain and Turkey in my fighter pilot days I was intrigued by shepherds tending their flocks 24/7 on the open range in a manner unchanged in the two millennia since Jesus walked the earth. Sheep are perhaps the least intelligent of animals. In my agrarian youth, "Dumber than a hundred head of sheep" was the worst (and cruelest) thing you could say about another's intelligence. When on low-level training missions in my F-100 in central Turkey, the sound of my jet would scare flocks of grazing sheep. But instead of running helter-skelter to hide, they would all run to the center of the flock, creating a large woolly pile that must have killed at least a few of them. As I streaked by a hundred feet overhead the pile, I could see the angry shepherd shaking his fist at me. I do not blame him. I was grateful he was not aiming his ancient musket at me.

The relationship between dumb animal and shepherd is apparent to anyone who looks. While all sheep appear the same to me, a shepherd can tell them all apart and has a name for each of them. The sheep are dependent on their shepherd for literally everything they need to live and they seem to have a sense of that. They recognize his voice and know enough to follow him wherever he goes, but they will wander off mindlessly while grazing, so busy filling their bellies that they pay no attention to where they are. So it is in the relationship between born again believer and God.

The mental gap between sheep and human beings is enormous. It is an excellent illustration of the gap between the mind of man and the mind of God, though in reality the gap for the latter is infinite.

This brief sketch on animal husbandry makes it plain why sheep provided Jesus' favorite metaphor. It also explains why I find this fifth unshakable certainty so rich in illuminating imagery, so profoundly heartwarming, so unshakably assuring.

My sheep listen to my voice; I know them, and they follow me. I give them eternal life, and they shall never perish; no one can snatch them out of my hand (John 10:27-28).

Jesus was, as always when he talked, speaking for the ages when he made this wonderful promise.

But the context was another tense confrontation with the Pharisees. Earlier, in Jerusalem, Jesus had caused quite a stir by healing a man who had been blind since birth (John 9:1-7). For most of his life the man had been a blind beggar in the Temple courtyard and was known by many. The news spread like wildfire. The Pharisees launched a full-scale investigation, hoping to prove it was some kind of hoax, but witnesses were hesitant to talk. Everyone knew that anyone who acknowledged that Jesus was the Messiah ("Christ" in Greek) would be excommunicated from the synagogue. So the Pharisees grilled the happy man, who at that point did not know who it was that had healed him. He said, "One thing I do know. I was blind but now I see!" They continued to ask him a lot of sinister questions that made him angry. He had just been the recipient of a wonderful miracle and these pontificating Pharisees were trying to make something evil out of it. In spite of his former blindness he argued like a learned man. He said, "Nobody has ever heard of opening the eyes of a man born blind. If this man were not from God, he could do nothing" (John 9:32-33).

Such a truth thrown in their faces by an uneducated beggar really set off the Pharisees. They threw him out of the synagogue.

When Jesus heard about it he went looking for the man. He found him in Solomon's Portico, the magnificent covered, colonnaded hallway that ran the entire length, longer than four football fields, of the eastern wall of the Temple compound. It was a popular meeting area that accommodated thousands, with a spectacular view of the one-hundred-fifty-foot high white marble, gold-trimmed Temple in the middle of the courtyard and a panoramic westerly view of the Mount of Olives a mile away across the Kidron Valley.

> *Jesus said, "Do you believe in the Son of Man?" "Who is he, sir?" the man asked. "Tell me so that I may believe in him" (John 9:35b-36).*

Jesus called himself the Son of Man many times, and by this time his reputation had grown throughout the land – the man who claims to be the Son of God and calls himself the Son of Man. The blind man, who had spent his life begging in the Temple area, would have had a heightened sense of hearing, as blind people do to compensate, and must have heard all the talk, both pro and con about Jesus. He would have been very familiar with the term, Son of Man.

> *Jesus said, "You have now seen him; in fact, he is the one speaking with you." Then the man said, "Lord, I believe," and he worshipped him (John 9:37-38).*

Can you imagine a more thrilling moment in your earthly life?

Apparently the Pharisees had been tailing the former blind man, or Jesus, or both, because they overheard their conversation. So for their burning ears Jesus said, "For judgment I have come into this world, so that the blind will see and those who see will become blind" (John 9:39).

The objective of Jesus coming into the world was to present the good news of salvation by grace, not works, and confront people with their obligation to decide for or against him. Those who are blind to his truth but become spiritually reborn by his grace will see that truth. Those conceited souls who falsely think they have special wisdom through their own unregenerate interpretation of the things of God become blind to divine revelation.

"What? Are we blind too?" (John 9:40) the Pharisees asked in a rage.

That launched Jesus into his sermon using his favorite metaphor – sheep. He ignored their rage and talked to them as if they were all his favorite children. "I am the good shepherd. The good shepherd lays down his life for the sheep" (John 10:11).

Their sinful minds comprehended neither the figurative nor literal truth with which Jesus spoke, but it would not be long before they would see with their own eyes the proof of the truthfulness of this promise, as Jesus lay down his life on the cross.

Then he made another promise that went over their heads as well. They thought only they were God's special people, which, until Jesus came, they were. "I have other sheep that are not of this sheep pen. I must bring them also. They too will listen to my voice, and there shall be one flock and one shepherd" (John 10:16).

Jesus was talking about non-Jewish believers, those the Jews called Gentiles, who would also be called to spiritual rebirth. That, of course, has come to pass beginning shortly after his death and resurrection, when the Apostle Paul, among others, traveled far and wide bringing the gospel to Gentiles in the Roman world. Today the "other sheep" who believe in Jesus far exceed those who are ethnically Jewish, but God's plan is not yet fulfilled, and will not be till Jesus comes again.

It was during a Jewish holiday that is now called Hanukkah when Jesus once again confronted perhaps these same Pharisees in the same place – Solomon's Portico. They were always trying to show off their superior knowledge, but in this case they were also trying to trap Jesus into saying something self-incriminating with which they could prosecute him before the Roman authorities. Like good lawyers they were trying to get him to quit talking in parables and state simply and clearly that he was the Messiah. They needed unequivocal evidence. The Pharisees and most Jews thought the Old Testament prophecies of a Messiah meant a political leader who would come to throw off the chains of Roman bondage and usher in the glory days of Kings David and Solomon. In spite of all the times Jesus had interpreted the Law and the Prophets in his sermons, patiently explaining how the prophecies, over 250 of them, called for a spiritual deliverer, a suffering servant who would save them from sin and death, they remained obstinate. In spite of all his miracles, they, in their blindness and jealousy, thought he was a fraud. They thought that if they could get him to say he was the Messiah before so many witnesses, they could bring their case to Pilate, accusing Jesus of plotting to overthrow the Roman rule of Israel. Treason. End of case. End of troublemaker.

Jesus saw through it all.

The Jews gathered around him, saying, "How long will you keep us in suspense? If you are the Christ, tell us plainly."

Jesus answered, "I did tell you, but you do not believe. The miracles I do in my Father's name speak for me, but you do not believe because you are not my sheep. My sheep listen to my voice; I know them, and they follow me. I give them eternal

*life, and they shall never perish; no one can snatch
them out of my hand" (John 10:24-28).*

There in the midst of that tense debate Jesus
delivers the most comforting words a Christian
could ever hear – "no one can snatch them out
of my hand." He also implies again God's secret
will for determining who gets mercifully born again
spiritually. He says, "you do not believe because
you are not my sheep." Those hearts God does
not regenerate cannot see the things of God and
will not be drawn to belief in Jesus Christ – the
first and second unshakable certainties. Only God
knows who his sheep are, past, present and future.
We can make some assumptions about who they
are among our contemporaries, based on how
they live their lives, by the fruit they bear as born
again children of God, but only our Lord knows for
sure. When we get to heaven we will probably be
surprised at whom we see there ...and whom we
do not see.

The palm of God's hand is a powerful image of
blessed assurance. There is nothing so sweet in all
the world as knowing God loves you, knowing with
conviction he has guaranteed your eternal life,
knowing with certainty you reside securely in the
all-powerful palm of his hand and knowing with
confidence that no one can ever remove you. This
eternal security for God's people is a wonderful
state of grace. You cannot be snatched away. You
cannot jump out of his palm – he has inclined your
will against it. You may backslide, you will still sin
as the born again self battles the residue of sin
from the old self in this earthly life, but you will
repent and God will forgive you. David, a man
after God's own heart, committed adultery and

murder, and when confronted with it by Nathan his spiritual advisor, he fell on his face and begged God's forgiveness (Ps. 51). God forgave him, and according to his plan for all his chosen people David did not lose his salvation (though he did pay for that terrible sin the rest of his life with a chaotic home life). Even the Apostle Paul wrestled with the sins of the old self. He confessed to his friends in Rome,

I do not understand what I do. For what I want to do I do not do, but what I hate I do. ... As it is, it is no longer I myself who do it, but it is sin living in me. I know that nothing good lives in me, that is, in my sinful nature. For I have the desire to do what is good, but I cannot carry it out. For what I do is not the good I want to do; no, the evil I do not want to do – this I keep on doing. ... So I find this law at work: When I want to do good, evil is right there with me (Romans 7:15, 17-19, 21).

God does not promise a bed of roses in the security of his divine palm, as David, Paul and this writer can attest. He will not spare the rod on those children he loves if they are deserving of it, because it is for their own good.

Paul said, "And we know that in all things God works for the good of those who love him" (Romans 8:28).

He may challenge us to do great things for his glory in hard conditions, but we are safe ...forever safe ...eternally secure. Again the eloquent Paul speaks to this: "[He] ...is able to keep you from falling and to present you before his glorious presence without fault and with great joy" (Jude 24).

The Good Shepherd's sheep never had it so good. Do you know his voice?

*No one can see the kingdom of God
unless he is born again.
No one can come to me unless the Father
who sent me draws him.
No one comes to the Father except through me.
No one takes it [life] from me, but I lay it down
of my own accord.
No one can snatch them out of my hand.
(John 3:3; 6:44; 14:6; 10:18; 10:28.)*

These are unshakable certainties in an uncertain world.

6

The Sixth Unshakable Certainty

No one will take away your joy (John 16:22b).

This sixth unshakable certainty from the mouth of Jesus is a natural conclusion to the first five that we have been studying. When God initiates his plan of salvation in a person, he will complete it. If he regenerates the heart of a sinner so that he can see the things of God, he will draw him irresistibly to his son, Jesus Christ, who purchased his salvation on the cross, and through the work of the Holy Spirit will escort him through this life to the glory of the Father's presence. And he will be as secure in that process as if he were living in the loving hand of God himself. That is joy unspeakable. C. H. Spurgeon said, "No greater happiness is possible." Jesus promised no one can take that away.

In studying God's Word the historical setting as well as the actual circumstances are critical to a right understanding. That is particularly true in this sixth unshakable certainty spoken by Jesus. Enroute to the Mount of Olives from the upper room with his disciples, the night air seemed full of foreboding and confusion to the disciples. Jesus talked at length about what would happen next. It was weighty stuff and again the disciples struggled to understand.

Jesus explained that when he returned to the right hand of God in the heavenly throne room they would not be left alone. The Father and the Son would send a "counselor," the Holy Spirit – the third person of the Triune God – to be with them (John 16:7). Jesus said, "when he, the Spirit of truth, comes, he will guide you into all truth" (John 16:13a).

That is the same Holy Spirit that works in born again Christians to enable them to see the things of God, draws them to Christ, and inclines their will to do God's will.

Then he said, "In a little while you will see me no more, and then after a little while you will see me" (John 16:16).

He meant that because of his death and burial within a day they would not see him for a while. (We know in hindsight that it was three days.) Then when he rose from the dead they would see him again. They were still addled. It is hard for us, having read the whole story, to see how the disciples could be so uncomprehending after all they had lived through with Jesus. But these were common men, fishermen, tradesmen, and tax collectors, not scholars. It makes it all the more remarkable to see the change that came over them on the day of Pentecost about seven weeks later, when the Holy Spirit descended on them in tongues of fire. They were transformed into bold, bright, articulate yet humble men who heroically proclaimed the gospel of Jesus Christ and changed the world.

Jesus saw they were confused and without giving them any more details he told them they would soon go through a time of grieving. He said, "I tell you the truth, you will weep and mourn while the [unbelieving] world rejoices. You will grieve, but your grief will turn to joy."

He likened their pain to a woman going through the pain of childbirth who then rejoices at the birth of her child. He said, "So with you: Now is your time of grief, but I will see you again and you will rejoice, and no one will take away your joy" (John 16:22).

In other words, they will grieve because of his crucifixion but rejoice when they see and realize he has risen from the dead. He will defeat death, a truly extraordinary thing – a miracle of the highest order. Joy indeed! That is the same joy that still fills a born again Christian today, two thousand years later – the joy of earthly life secure in destiny, come what may, joy beyond the meaning of words, beyond the comprehension of mere mortals, that will be ours in heaven. The world cannot rob us of that joy nor the treasure in heaven that awaits us. Nothing and no one can separate us from the love of Christ who died for his people. Perhaps the Apostle Paul painted the best picture. He said,

> For I am convinced that neither death nor life, neither angels nor demons, neither the present nor the future, nor any powers, neither height nor depth, nor anything else in all creation, will be able to separate us from the love of God that is in Christ Jesus our Lord (Rom 8:38-39).

Had Paul taken a lesson from Jesus he could have said, "I am convinced that nothing will be able to separate us..." and saved two dozen words, but we would have lost a masterpiece of a word picture. We could title it "JOY."

All this was planned and executed for the sinner who wrote this book, who was content to wallow in the mud of his sin, oblivious to his peril. I do not deserve to be the husband of the beautiful, loving lady who consented to be my wife forty years ago. She loves me still in spite of just cause to hate me. How much more miraculous that a gracious God could love me when I was unlovable, rebellious, ignorant of the things of God and utterly unmotivated to learn. And lo these years he has sanctified me – brought me ever closer to him – but I am still more a lump of coal than a diamond. One day I shall shine like that diamond, though, as I reflect his presence in glory. It is that undeserved joy, that inner "peace of God that transcends all understanding" (Phil. 4:7) in an uncertain world that bears witness to the Holy Spirit that dwells within. The fruit of that Spirit is "love, joy, peace, patience, kindness, goodness, faithfulness, gentleness and self-control" (Gal. 5:22-23). Some days the fruit I bear is rotten, other days it is barely passable. Often, in my impatience, it falls before it is ripe. But God has promised he will not give up on me. When my regenerated heart makes it plain to my still selfish old self that I have sinned against the great God who loves me, I beg forgiveness. He is gracious and kind to forgive me of my sins, because when he looks at me he sees my Savior Jesus, my mediator with God the Father day and night (1 Tim. 2:5) and my advocate on Judgment Day when I will be too overwhelmed to talk. Such a secure future is a joy even when I am having a bad day. All else in life is just trivial details compared to the unsurpassing love of Christ that is and will forever be mine.

So how should we then live? In delightful gratitude!

I live in joyful wonder and amazement at a holy God who hates sin yet loves this sinner so much he has rescued me from my hell-bound madness! It is gratitude that leads me to cheerfully do good works for God's kingdom, not a desire to build a resumé for Judgment Day that will be worthless anyway. It is gratitude that leads me to wrestle daily with the old self, to strive to live up to the impossible standard of the Ten Commandants. It is gratitude that joyfully drives me fifteen miles out of my beloved mountains and into town for church twice on Sundays and once on Wednesdays. It is gratitude that drives me to my knees when I fail to glorify the God in whom I live and breathe and have my being. It is gratitude that drives me to bear good fruit of the Spirit. It is heartfelt gratitude that drives me to sing John Newton's hymn with gusto,

> *Amazing Grace, how sweet the sound,*
> *that saved a wretch like me.*

And even this joy is God's gift – the Holy Spirit has inclined my will and motivated my gratitude. This is what glorifies God and allows me to enjoy him forever.

The word "joy," which embodies so much meaning in just three letters, appears 217 times in the Bible, which should say a great deal to those people who say Christians have no fun. In 1643 a group of 151 learned English Christians, three-quarters of whom were preachers, set about at the direction of Parliament to write a doctrinal statement that distilled all that God had to say in the Bible. Four years later they presented Parliament with *The Westminster Confession of Faith*, *The Larger Catechism*, and *The Shorter Catechism*. A catechism is a set of questions and answers, like "Frequently Asked Questions" at a website, that explain in concise terms a religious doctrine. In this case *The Shorter Catechism* was for teaching children. Every phrase in every sentence in all three documents was footnoted with supporting scripture references.

The first question in *The Shorter Catechism* is "What is the chief end of man?" The answer, taking into account all the joy expounded in the Bible, is, "Man's chief end is to glorify God and enjoy him forever." The primary reason for our existence, the answer to the eternal question that is in the mind of every human who ever drew a breath, is to glorify God and enjoy him and his magnificent creation forever. *The Westminster Confession* is part of the official doctrine of a number of Protestant denominations today, though, sadly, few in the pews know of it or its doctrinal claims.

The Westminster divines had a large table piled high with source books and various Bible translations at their disposal in the anteroom of their Westminster Abbey meeting room. One of those source books was another catechism written a hundred years earlier by Heidelberg resident Zacharias Ursinus, a student of Dr. Martin Luther, the great reformer. The first question of the *Heidelberg Catechism* is equally weighty and much longer but with a similar intent as *The Westminster Catechism's* first question. It eloquently embodies the "No one" sayings of Jesus.

Q. What is your only comfort in life and death?

A. That I, with body and soul, both in life and death, am not my own, but belong unto my faithful Savior Jesus Christ; who with his precious blood has fully satisfied for all my sins, and delivered me from all the power of the devil; and so preserves me that without the will of my heavenly Father not a hair can fall from my head; yea, that all things must be subservient to my salvation, wherefore by his Holy Spirit He also assures me of eternal life, and makes me heartily willing and ready, henceforth, to live unto him.

The word "joy" does not appear here, but passionate joy is felt in every phrase, joy that engenders a grateful heart.

Both the Westminster and the Heidelberg catechisms were written at a time when religion was taken much more seriously than it is in our culture as a whole. People were persecuted for their faith, and no one professed his beliefs without knowing that he could end up being killed for it. Heretics were burned at the stake. Heresy was by definition "half-truth," so you could die in the sixteenth and seventeenth centuries for being only half-wrong, according to the authorities.

A devout group in England, who lived by *The Westminster Confession* before it was even codified, chose to emigrate to the dangerous new frontier in North America where they could live their faith and raise their families free from religious persecution. They thought the state of their eternal souls was of more importance than life itself, and they were willing to risk death and disease and brutal hardships in a strange land far away to properly practice their religion. They were called Puritans, a term that applied to a broad body of Protestant denominations in England, the largest of which was Presbyterian (half the Westminster divines were Presbyterians). The name was derived from their intense desire to purify the Church of England of practices not prescribed in the Bible. The United States of America owes the Puritans a great debt. Its government, one of the world's longest running and most successful experiments in self-government by free people, is based on their precepts. Dr. Martin Marty, retired Professor of Religious History at the University of Chicago, calls our system a "Presbyterian form of government." The Puritans founded some of our greatest universities.

The Puritans believed that the Reformation of the previous century, initiated by Martin Luther in Germany, and carried on by John Calvin in Geneva and John Knox in Scotland, had brought Christianity back to the pure faith and doctrine espoused by the Bible writers and especially Jesus himself. It began providentially – God was in charge of the details back then too. Luther, in an effort to get a dialogue going with church authorities, nailed ninety-five debating points to the bulletin board (which doubled as the church door) of the castle church at Wittenburg, Germany on what we now call Halloween Day, 1517. Through a series of ever more volatile exchanges with the Church of Rome, it led to a showdown at the Diet of Worms, the rough equivalent of today's United Nations, on April 18, 1521. Luther stood before the assembled heads of Europe and was asked to recant his writings, stacked on a table in front of him. They were the very writings that led to the Westminster and Heidelberg catechisms. To refuse to recant meant death and everyone in the room knew it. Luther refused. He said,

> Unless I am convinced by the testimony of Sacred Scripture or by evident reason...my conscience is captive to the word of God. I cannot and I will not recant anything, for to go against my conscience is neither right nor safe. Here I stand. I can do no other. God help me. Amen.

British historian Thomas Carlyle called it, "The greatest moment in the modern history of man." The Reformation Martin Luther ignited because he feared God more than man did indeed change the world. He avoided capture through the aid of his friendly king, Frederick the Wise of Saxony, but he lived under a death sentence from Rome the rest of his life – twenty-eight years. The Reformation spread like wildfire across Europe and England, aided immeasurably by the providential recent invention of the printing press and Luther's voluminous writings. It then leaped the Atlantic Ocean to the New World, carried in the born again hearts of Puritan pilgrims on fire for the kingdom of God. Like Luther, they were willing to stake their lives on the "No one" statements, the unshakable certainties proclaimed by Jesus Christ.

Now, after four centuries in America, the faith of our fathers has been diluted, distorted and marginalized. It has been corrupted by the secular humanists, the modernists and now the post modernists, all failed worldviews held by people who have not had their hearts regenerated by the grace of God. Except for a few million believers, that faith has been divided and split and spun off and would be unrecognizable by any Puritan in the Plymouth Colony.

"No one..."

Today the Puritans of old have become a caricature for mean, miserable people by revisionist historians and popular novels and movies. "Puritan" has even become a disparaging colloquialism in our cruel culture, but nothing could be further from the truth. Any casual reading of Puritan literature will show they were joyful people, and they were joyful precisely because they believed the truths of God's Word with conviction as laid out in this little book and in the Westminster and Heidelberg catechisms.

If all who profess to be Christians would model their lives after the Puritans, with their love for God, their zealousness for his truth, their courage, piety and joy in the Lord, then we could arrest this culture's sleepwalking parade to perdition and reform the world.

It is good to know the heart of role models, and how better to know a Puritan heart than to read its earnest prayer?

O Supreme Moving Cause,
may I always be subordinate to thee,
be dependent upon thee,
be found in the path where thou dost walk
and where thy Spirit moves,
take heed of estrangement from thee,
of becoming insensible to thy love.
Thou dost not move men like stones,
but dost endue them with life,
not to enable them to move without thee,
but in submission to thee, the first mover.
O Lord, I am astonished at the difference
between my receivings and my deservings,
the state I am in now and my past gracelessness,
between the heaven I am bound for and the hell
I merit.

Who made me to differ, but thee?
For I was no more ready to receive Christ than were others;
I could not have begun to love thee hadst thou not first loved me,
Or been willing unless thou hadst first made me so.
O that such a crown should fit the head of such a sinner!
Such high advancement be for an unfruitful person!
Such joys for so vile a rebel!
Infinite wisdom cast the design of salvation
Into the mold of purchase and freedom;
Let wrath deserved be written on the door of hell,
But the free gift of grace on the door of heaven.
I know that my sufferings are the result of my sinning,
But in heaven both shall cease;
Grant me to attain this haven and be done with sailing,
And may the gales of thy mercy blow me safely into harbour.
Let thy love draw me nearer to thyself,
Wean me from sin, mortify me to this world,
And make me ready for my departure hence.
Secure me by thy grace as I sail across this stormy sea.[1]

Dear merciful God, teach me to pray like my Puritan brother of old... Did you note the joy? The gratitude?

To know the joy that no one can ever take away is the sixth unshakable certainty proclaimed by Jesus Christ. All six parts are inseparable. Together they add up to God's plan for the salvation of sinners, something utterly unachievable on our own. He leaves nothing to chance. He exercises his Lordship throughout, controlling every detail of every step. There is not a chance that we will

fall out of his hand. And there is no true
happiness except in the palm of his hand.

> *No one can see the kingdom of God*
> *unless he is born again.*
> *No one can come to me unless the Father*
> *who sent me draws him.*
> *No one comes to the Father except through me*
> *No one takes it [life] from me, but I lay it down*
> *of my own accord.*
> *No one can snatch them out of my hand.*
> *No one will take away your joy.*
> *(John 3:3; 6:44; 14:6; 10:18; 10:28; 16:22b)*

These are unshakable certainties in an uncertain
world, promises of God that are concise, crystal
clear, direct and personal. They comprise the faith
of our fathers, the bedrock of the Puritan worldview
and they are my worldview. Here I stand... but not
alone. I stand on the shoulders of giants, in the
palm of God's own hand.

You can take these "No one" sayings of Jesus and
torture the syntax and redefine words and perhaps
make them say something else so they will fit into
your preconceived worldview, but they will not be
God's unshakable certainties. You can choose to
ignore them, but at your own peril. Or you could
conclude that Jesus was a whole lot more than just
a nice guy and one day soon you'll have to give this
whole weighty matter some serious thought. And
then an airliner could fly through your office....

For the sake of your eternal soul, ask God for a
miracle. Ask him to change your heart and open
your eyes to his truth. He will do the rest and you
will learn who made you to differ from those who
never asked. Do it now. Always, always do it now.

No eye has seen, no ear has heard, no mind has conceived what God has prepared for those who love him (1 Cor. 2:9).

ENDNOTES

1. *The Valley of Vision: A collection of Puritan Prayers and devotions*, Arth Bennet (Ed.), Edinburgh and Carlisle, PA: The Banner of Truth Trust, 1975, page 8.

Appendix 1:
The Things That Matter

If George Barna's opinion polls have accurately taken the measure of religious belief in America, then there is at least a 95 percent chance that, even if you are a regular church attendee in America, you've never heard the truths expounded in this book in your church.[1] The Barna Group defines a biblical worldview the same way I do, as requiring

> ...someone to believe that absolute moral truth exists; that the source of moral truth is the Bible; that the Bible is accurate in all of the principles it teaches; that eternal spiritual salvation cannot be earned; that Jesus lived a sinless life on earth; that every person has a responsibility to share their religious beliefs with others; that Satan is a living force, not just a symbol of evil; and that God is the all-knowing, all-powerful maker of the universe who still rules that creation today.

In spite of the fact that 88 percent of those polled felt "accepted by God," 82 percent said they were "clear about the meaning and purpose" of their life, and 62 percent considered themselves to be "deeply spiritual," only 5 percent of adults had a biblical worldview. Barna's research led to the following recommendation, when asked for ideas as to how to remedy this widespread ignorance of biblical principles:

> *We know that within two hours after leaving a church service, the typical individual cannot recall the theme of the sermon they heard. But if they have a discussion about a principle and its application to their life, or if they have a multi-sensory experience with those principles, they retain the information much longer and the probability that they will act on that information rises dramatically.*

George Barna concluded his findings with a reminder to "Christian leaders to stay focused on the things that matter." The six unshakable certainties declared by Jesus Christ are the only things that ultimately matter. Therefore I urge you to form a small group of your friends to discuss these eternal truths using the wealth of supporting scripture contained in Appendix 2.

This is not an effort to create the newest new fad in spirituality, or the latest xx-day discovery plan of who you are and why you are here. It is an effort to indelibly imprint the most important message the mind can receive – how God saves sinners – in your gray matter using Barna's suggestions. This is a small book and the six unshakable certainties from the Son of God's own lips are easier to memorize than almost anything. With perhaps an introductory discussion session followed by one chapter per meeting and a concluding session, it could be done in eight meetings (eight days or eight weeks) – hopefully well within the attention span of any serious Christian or "seeker." Further meetings could focus on writing a personal presentation like the gospel manuscript in the model of Appendix 3. In my early days as a wannabe writer, I met with a group of like-minded folks regularly to read and critique and mutually support one another's work. It was invaluable. Overlay it all with group prayer for one another. The greatest privilege we have this side of heaven is to come into the presence of God in prayer.

As an aid to memorizing these six scripture verses, I have created a Word file that prints "portrait" style on both sides of a business card, creating a book mark with the six unshakable certainties printed on it, using Avery #5376 or #5876 card stock. Email me through my website at www.jdwetterling.com and click on "Email JD" and I shall be happy to send it to you.

ENDNOTES

---

1. "Most Adults Feel Accepted by God, But Lack a Biblical Worldview," August 9, 2005. http://www.barna.org/FlexPage. aspx?Page=BarnaUpdateNarrow&BarnaUpdateID=194

Appendix 2:
For further study

There is a vast body of Scripture specifically supporting Jesus' "No one" declarations besides those given in this book. Taken as a whole they are often referred to as the Doctrines of Grace. This is a summary of scripture supporting five aspects (also known as The Canons of Dort) of the Doctrines of Grace as preached by Jesus and all the gospel writers in the Bible.[1]

I.   Natural man is never able to do any good that is fundamentally pleasing to God, including believing in him, and in fact, does evil all the time. This is the clear witness of Scripture.

II. God chooses some to go to heaven, but his choice is never based on what man thinks, says, does, is or what God foresees in that man's thoughts, words and deeds. We do not know what God bases his choice on, but it is not anything that is in man.

III. Atonement, which is unlimited in its power, is limited to a definite, particular number of people, namely those God chose for saving faith in Him.

IV. When God sends his Holy Spirit to those he has chosen, they cannot resist him.

V. Once saved, always saved – "the grandest thought in the Bible. Once you believe you can never be lost, you can never go to hell."[2]

I. Natural man is never able to do any good that is fundamentally pleasing to God, including believing in him, and in fact, does evil all the time. This is the clear witness of Scripture.

SCRIPTURE PROOFS
Ephesians 2:1-3
As for you, you were dead in your transgressions and sins, in which you used to live when you followed the ways of this world and of the ruler of the kingdom of the air, the spirit who is now at work in those who are disobedient. All of us also lived among them at one time, gratifying the cravings of our sinful nature and following its desires and thoughts. Like the rest, we were by nature objects of wrath.

Colossians. 2:13
When you were dead in your sins and in the uncircumcision of your sinful nature, God made you alive with Christ. He forgave us all our sins.

Genesis 2:16-17
And the LORD God commanded the man, "You are free to eat from any tree in the garden; but you must not eat from the tree of the knowledge of good and evil, for when you eat of it you will surely die."

Genesis 6:5
The LORD saw how great man's wickedness on the earth had become, and that every inclination of the thoughts of his heart was only evil all the time.

Genesis 8:21
The LORD smelled the pleasing aroma and said in his heart: "Never again will I curse the ground because of man, even though every inclination of his heart is

evil from childhood. And never again will I destroy all living creatures, as I have done."

Ecclesiastes 9:3
This is the evil in everything that happens under the sun: The same destiny overtakes all. The hearts of men, moreover, are full of evil and there is madness in their hearts while they live, and afterward they join the dead.

Jeremiah 17:9
The heart is deceitful above all things and beyond cure. Who can understand it?

Mark 7:21-23
For from within, out of men's hearts, come evil thoughts, sexual immorality, theft, murder, adultery, greed, malice, deceit, lewdness, envy, slander, arrogance and folly. All these evils come from inside and make a man 'unclean.'

John 8:44
You belong to your father, the devil, and you want to carry out your father's desire. He was a murderer from the beginning, not holding to the truth, for there is no truth in him. When he lies, he speaks his native language, for he is a liar and the father of lies.

2 Timothy 2:25-26
Those who oppose him he must gently instruct, in the hope that God will grant them repentance leading them to a knowledge of the truth, and that they will come to their senses and escape from the trap of the devil, who has taken them captive to do his will.

1 John 3:10
This is how we know who the children of God are and who the children of the devil are: Anyone who does not do what is right is not a child of God; nor is anyone who does not love his brother.

1 John 5:19
We know that we are children of God, and that the whole world is under the control of the evil one.

Romans 6:20
When you were slaves to sin, you were free from the control of righteousness.

Titus 3:3
At one time we too were foolish, disobedient, deceived and enslaved by all kinds of passions and pleasures. We lived in malice and envy, being hated and hating one another.

John 3:3
In reply Jesus declared, "I tell you the truth, no one can see the kingdom of God unless he is born again."

John 6:44
"No one can come to me unless the Father who sent me draws him, and I will raise him up at the last day."

John 6:65
He went on to say, "This is why I told you that no one can come to me unless the Father has enabled him."

Romans 8:7-8
The sinful mind is hostile to God. It does not submit to God's law, nor can it do so. Those controlled by the sinful nature cannot please God.

1 Corinthians 2:14
The man without the Spirit does not accept the things that come from the Spirit of God, for they are foolishness to him, and he cannot understand them, because they are spiritually discerned.

Romans 3:9-12
What shall we conclude then? Are we any better? Not at all! We have already made the charge that Jews

and Gentiles alike are all under sin. As it is written: "There is no one righteous, not even one; there is no one who understands, no one who seeks God. All have turned away, they have together become worthless; there is no one who does good, not even one."

II. God chooses some to go to heaven, but his choice is never based on what man thinks, says, does, is or what God foresees in that man's thoughts, words and deeds. We do not know what God bases his choice on, but it is not anything that is in man.

SCRIPTURE PROOFS
Deuteronomy 10:14-15
To the LORD your God belong the heavens, even the highest heavens, the earth and everything in it. Yet the LORD set his affection on your forefathers and loved them, and he chose you, their descendants, above all the nations, as it is today.

Matthew 24:22
If those days had not been cut short, no one would survive, but for the sake of the elect those days will be shortened.

Matthew 24:24
For false Christs and false prophets will appear and perform great signs and miracles to deceive even the elect – if that were possible.

Matthew 24:31
And he will send his angels with a loud trumpet call, and they will gather his elect from the four winds, from one end of the heavens to the other.

John 6:37-39
All that the Father gives me will come to me, and whoever comes to me I will never drive away. For

I have come down from heaven not to do my will but to do the will of him who sent me. And this is the will of him who sent me, that I shall lose none of all that he has given me, but raise them up at the last day.

John 6:65
He went on to say, "This is why I told you that no one can come to me unless the Father has enabled him."

John 17:9
I pray for them. I am not praying for the world, but for those you have given me, for they are yours.

Romans 8:28-33
And we know that in all things God works for the good of those who love him, who have been called according to his purpose. For those God foreknew he also predestined to be conformed to the likeness of his Son, that he might be the firstborn among many brothers. And those he predestined, he also called; those he called, he also justified; those he justified, he also glorified. What, then, shall we say in response to this? If God is for us, who can be against us? He who did not spare his own Son, but gave him up for us all – how will he not also, along with him, graciously give us all things? Who will bring any charge against those whom God has chosen? It is God who justifies.

Romans 11:5
So too, at the present time there is a remnant chosen by grace.

Ephesians 1:4-5
For he chose us in him before the creation of the world to be holy and blameless in his sight. In love he predestined us to be adopted as his sons through Jesus Christ, in accordance with his pleasure and will.

Ephesians 1:11
In him we were also chosen, having been predestined
according to the plan of him who works out everything
in conformity with the purpose of his will.

1 Thessalonians 1:4-5
For we know, brothers loved by God, that he has
chosen you, because our gospel came to you not
simply with words, but also with power, with the Holy
Spirit and with deep conviction. You know how we
lived among you for your sake.

1 Thessalonians 5:9
For God did not appoint us to suffer wrath but to
receive salvation through our Lord Jesus Christ.

1 Peter 1:1-2
Peter, an apostle of Jesus Christ, To God's elect,
strangers in the world, scattered throughout Pontus,
Galatia, Cappadocia, Asia and Bithynia, who have
been chosen according to the foreknowledge of God
the Father, through the sanctifying work of the Spirit,
for obedience to Jesus Christ and sprinkling by his
blood: Grace and peace be yours in abundance.

1 Peter 2:8-9
"A stone that causes men to stumble and a rock that
makes them fall." They stumble because they disobey
the message – which is also what they were destined
for. But you are a chosen people, a royal priesthood,
a holy nation, a people belonging to God, that you
may declare the praises of him who called you out of
darkness into his wonderful light.

Deuteronomy 7:6-8
For you are a people holy to the LORD your God. The
LORD your God has chosen you out of all the peoples
on the face of the earth to be his people, his treasured
possession. The LORD did not set his affection on you
and choose you because you were more numerous
than other peoples, for you were the fewest of all

peoples. But it was because the L ord loved you and kept the oath he swore to your forefathers that he brought you out with a mighty hand and redeemed you from the land of slavery, from the power of Pharaoh king of Egypt.

Romans 9:11-13
Yet, before the twins were born or had done anything good or bad – in order that God's purpose in election might stand: not by works but by him who calls – she was told, "The older will serve the younger." Just as it is written: "Jacob I loved, but Esau I hated."

Romans 9:16
It does not, therefore, depend on man's desire or effort, but on God's mercy.

1 Corinthians 1:27-29
But God chose the foolish things of the world to shame the wise; God chose the weak things of the world to shame the strong. He chose the lowly things of this world and the despised things – and the things that are not – to nullify the things that are, so that no one may boast before him.

2 Timothy 1:9
[He] has saved us and called us to a holy life – not because of anything we have done but because of his own purpose and grace. This grace was given us in Christ Jesus before the beginning of time.

Acts 13:48
When the Gentiles heard this, they were glad and honored the word of the Lord; and all who were appointed for eternal life believed.

Acts 18:27
When Apollos wanted to go to Achaia, the brothers encouraged him and wrote to the disciples there to welcome him. On arriving, he was a great help to those who by grace had believed.

Ephesians 2:10
For we are God's workmanship, created in Christ
Jesus to do good works, which God prepared in
advance for us to do.

Philippians 1:29
For it has been granted to you on behalf of Christ not
only to believe on him, but also to suffer for him.

Philippians 2:13
For it is God who works in you to will and to act
according to his good purpose.

1 Thessalonians 1:4-5
For we know, brothers loved by God, that he has
chosen you, because our gospel came to you not
simply with words, but also with power, with the Holy
Spirit and with deep conviction. You know how we
lived among you for your sake.

2 Thessalonians 2:13-14
But we ought always to thank God for you, brothers
loved by the Lord, because from the beginning God
chose you to be saved through the sanctifying work
of the Spirit and through belief in the truth. He called
you to this through our gospel, that you might share
in the glory of our Lord Jesus Christ.

2 Peter 1:5-11
For this very reason, make every effort to add to
your faith goodness; and to goodness, knowledge;
and to knowledge, self-control; and to self-control,
perseverance; and to perseverance, godliness; and
to godliness, brotherly kindness; and to brotherly
kindness, love. For if you possess these qualities in
increasing measure, they will keep you from being
ineffective and unproductive in your knowledge of our
Lord Jesus Christ. But if anyone does not have them,
he is nearsighted and blind, and has forgotten that he
has been cleansed from his past sins. Therefore, my
brothers, be all the more eager to make your calling

and election sure. For if you do these things, you will never fall, and you will receive a rich welcome into the eternal kingdom of our Lord and Savior Jesus Christ.

Amos 3:2
You only have I chosen of all the families of the earth; therefore I will punish you for all your sins.

Jeremiah 1:5
Before I formed you in the womb I knew you, before you were born I set you apart; I appointed you as a prophet to the nations.

Matthew 7:22-23
Many will say to me on that day, "Lord, Lord, did we not prophesy in your name, and in your name drive out demons and perform many miracles?" Then I will tell them plainly, "I never knew you. Away from me, you evildoers!"

1 Corinthians 8:3
But the man who loves God is known by God.

2 Timothy 2:19
Nevertheless, God's solid foundation stands firm, sealed with this inscription: "The Lord knows those who are his," and, "Everyone who confesses the name of the Lord must turn away from wickedness."

1 Peter 1:20
He was chosen before the creation of the world, but was revealed in these last times for your sake.

III. Atonement, which is unlimited in its power, is limited to a definite, particular number of people, namely those God chose for saving faith in Him.

SCRIPTURE PROOFS
Romans 5:8-10
But God demonstrates his own love for us in this: While we were still sinners, Christ died for us. Since

we have now been justified by his blood, how much more shall we be saved from God's wrath through him! For if, when we were God's enemies, we were reconciled to him through the death of his Son, how much more, having been reconciled, shall we be saved through his life!

2 Corinthians 5:18-19
All this is from God, who reconciled us to himself through Christ and gave us the ministry of reconciliation: that God was reconciling the world to himself in Christ, not counting men's sins against them. And he has committed to us the message of reconciliation.

Ephesians 2:15-16
[He abolished] in his flesh the law with its commandments and regulations. His purpose was to create in himself one new man out of the two, thus making peace, and in this one body to reconcile both of them to God through the cross, by which he put to death their hostility.

Colossians 1:21-22
Once you were alienated from God and were enemies in your minds because of your evil behavior. But now he has reconciled you by Christ's physical body through death to present you holy in his sight, without blemish and free from accusation.

Luke 19:10
For the Son of Man came to seek and to save what was lost.

1 Timothy 1:15
Here is a trustworthy saying that deserves full acceptance: Christ Jesus came into the world to save sinners – of whom I am the worst.

John 6:35-40
Then Jesus declared, "I am the bread of life. He who comes to me will never go hungry, and he who

believes in me will never be thirsty. But as I told you, you have seen me and still you do not believe. All that the Father gives me will come to me, and whoever comes to me I will never drive away. For I have come down from heaven not to do my will but to do the will of him who sent me. And this is the will of him who sent me, that I shall lose none of all that he has given me, but raise them up at the last day. For my Father's will is that everyone who looks to the Son and believes in him shall have eternal life, and I will raise him up at the last day."

John 10:11
I am the good shepherd. The good shepherd lays down his life for the sheep.

John 10:14-18
I am the good shepherd; I know my sheep and my sheep know me – just as the Father knows me and I know the Father – and I lay down my life for the sheep. I have other sheep that are not of this sheep pen. I must bring them also. They too will listen to my voice, and there shall be one flock and one shepherd. The reason my Father loves me is that I lay down my life – only to take it up again. No one takes it from me, but I lay it down of my own accord. I have authority to lay it down and authority to take it up again. This command I received from my Father.

John 10:24-29
The Jews gathered around him, saying, "How long will you keep us in suspense? If you are the Christ, tell us plainly." Jesus answered, "I did tell you, but you do not believe. The miracles I do in my Father's name speak for me, but you do not believe because you are not my sheep. My sheep listen to my voice; I know them, and they follow me. I give them eternal life, and they shall never perish; no one can snatch them out of my hand. My Father, who has given them to me, is greater than all; no one can snatch them out of my Father's hand.

Ephesians 3:3-4

...the mystery [was] made known to me by revelation, as I have already written briefly. In reading this, then, you will be able to understand my insight into the mystery of Christ.

Ephesians 3:7

I became a servant of this gospel by the gift of God's grace given me through the working of his power.

John 17:1-11

After Jesus said this, he looked toward heaven and prayed: "Father, the time has come. Glorify your Son, that your Son may glorify you. For you granted him authority over all people that he might give eternal life to all those you have given him. Now this is eternal life: that they may know you, the only true God, and Jesus Christ, whom you have sent. I have brought you glory on earth by completing the work you gave me to do. And now, Father, glorify me in your presence with the glory I had with you before the world began. I have revealed you to those whom you gave me out of the world. They were yours; you gave them to me and they have obeyed your word. Now they know that everything you have given me comes from you. For I gave them the words you gave me and they accepted them. They knew with certainty that I came from you, and they believed that you sent me. I pray for them. I am not praying for the world, but for those you have given me, for they are yours. All I have is yours, and all you have is mine. And glory has come to me through them. I will remain in the world no longer, but they are still in the world, and I am coming to you. Holy Father, protect them by the power of your name – the name you gave me – so that they may be one as we are one."

John 17:20

My prayer is not for them alone. I pray also for those who will believe in me through their message.

John 17:24-26
Father, I want those you have given me to be with me where I am, and to see my glory, the glory you have given me because you loved me before the creation of the world. Righteous Father, though the world does not know you, I know you, and they know that you have sent me. I have made you known to them, and will continue to make you known in order that the love you have for me may be in them and that I myself may be in them.

Hebrews 2:17
For this reason he had to be made like his brothers in every way, in order that he might become a merciful and faithful high priest in service to God, and that he might make atonement for the sins of the people.

Hebrews 3:1
Therefore, holy brothers, who share in the heavenly calling, fix your thoughts on Jesus, the apostle and high priest whom we confess.

Hebrews 9:28
Christ was sacrificed once to take away the sins of many people; and he will appear a second time, not to bear sin, but to bring salvation to those who are waiting for him.

Revelation 5:9
And they sang a new song: "You are worthy to take the scroll and to open its seals, because you were slain, and with your blood you purchased men for God from every tribe and language and people and nation."

John 3:16-17
For God so loved the world that he gave his one and only Son, that whoever believes in him shall not perish but have eternal life. For God did not send his Son into the world to condemn the world, but to save the world through him.

2 Corinthians 5:19
God was reconciling the world to himself in Christ, not counting men's sins against them. And he has committed to us the message of reconciliation.

1 John 2:1-2
My dear children, I write this to you so that you will not sin. But if anybody does sin, we have one who speaks to the Father in our defense – Jesus Christ, the Righteous One. He is the atoning sacrifice for our sins, and not only for ours but also for the sins of the whole world.

1 John 4:14
And we have seen and testify that the Father has sent his Son to be the Savior of the world.

Romans 5:18
Consequently, just as the result of one trespass was condemnation for all men, so also the result of one act of righteousness was justification that brings life for all men.

2 Corinthians 5:14-15
For Christ's love compels us, because we are convinced that one died for all, and therefore all died. And he died for all, that those who live should no longer live for themselves but for him who died for them and was raised again.

1 Timothy 2:4-6
[He] wants all men to be saved and to come to a knowledge of the truth. For there is one God and one mediator between God and men, the man Christ Jesus, who gave himself as a ransom for all men – the testimony given in its proper time.

Hebrews 2:9
But we see Jesus, who was made a little lower than the angels, now crowned with glory and honor because he suffered death, so that by the grace of God he might taste death for everyone.

2 Peter 3:9
The Lord is not slow in keeping his promise, as some understand slowness. He is patient with you, not wanting anyone to perish, but everyone to come to repentance.

1 Corinthians 15:22
For as in Adam all die, so in Christ all will be made alive.

IV. When God sends his Holy Spirit to those he has chosen, they cannot resist him.

SCRIPTURE PROOFS
John 6:37
All that the Father gives me will come to me, and whoever comes to me I will never drive away.

John 6:44
No one can come to me unless the Father who sent me draws him, and I will raise him up at the last day.

John 10:16
I have other sheep that are not of this sheep pen. I must bring them also. They too will listen to my voice, and there shall be one flock and one shepherd.

Romans 8:29-30
For those God foreknew he also predestined to be conformed to the likeness of his Son, that he might be the firstborn among many brothers. And those he predestined, he also called; those he called, he also justified; those he justified, he also glorified.

Romans 8:32
He who did not spare his own Son, but gave him up for us all – how will he not also, along with him, graciously give us all things?

1 Corinthians 6:11
And that is what some of you were. But you were washed, you were sanctified, you were justified in

the name of the Lord Jesus Christ and by the Spirit of our God.

1 Corinthians 12:3
Therefore I tell you that no one who is speaking by the Spirit of God says, "Jesus be cursed," and no one can say, "Jesus is Lord," except by the Holy Spirit.

2 Corinthians 3:6
He has made us competent as ministers of a new covenant – not of the letter but of the Spirit; for the letter kills, but the Spirit gives life.

2 Corinthians 3:17-18
Now the Lord is the Spirit, and where the Spirit of the Lord is, there is freedom. And we, who with unveiled faces all reflect the Lord's glory, are being transformed into his likeness with ever-increasing glory, which comes from the Lord, who is the Spirit.

Ephesians 1:3-4
Praise be to the God and Father of our Lord Jesus Christ, who has blessed us in the heavenly realms with every spiritual blessing in Christ. For he chose us in him before the creation of the world to be holy and blameless in his sight. In love....

Ephesians 1:7
In him we have redemption through his blood, the forgiveness of sins, in accordance with the riches of God's grace

Ephesians 1:12
[We were chosen] in order that we, who were the first to hope in Christ, might be for the praise of his glory.

Ephesians 1:14
[The Holy Spirit] is a deposit guaranteeing our inheritance until the redemption of those who are God's possession – to the praise of his glory.

1 Peter 1:2
[God's elect] have been chosen according to the foreknowledge of God the Father, through the sanctifying work of the Spirit, for obedience to Jesus Christ and sprinkling by his blood: Grace and peace be yours in abundance.

A New Birth
John 1:12-13
Yet to all who received him, to those who believed in his name, he gave the right to become children of God – children born not of natural descent, nor of human decision or a husband's will, but born of God.

Romans 9:6
It is not as though God's word had failed. For not all who are descended from Israel are Israel.

John 3:3-8
In reply Jesus declared, "I tell you the truth, no one can see the kingdom of God unless he is born again." "How can a man be born when he is old?" Nicodemus asked. "Surely he cannot enter a second time into his mother's womb to be born!" Jesus answered, "I tell you the truth, no one can enter the kingdom of God unless he is born of water and the Spirit. Flesh gives birth to flesh, but the Spirit gives birth to spirit. You should not be surprised at my saying, 'You must be born again.' The wind blows wherever it pleases. You hear its sound, but you cannot tell where it comes from or where it is going. So it is with everyone born of the Spirit."

1 Peter 1:3
Praise be to the God and Father of our LORD Jesus Christ! In his great mercy he has given us new birth into a living hope through the resurrection of Jesus Christ from the dead.

1 John 5:4
For everyone born of God overcomes the world. This is the victory that has overcome the world, even our faith.

Titus 3:5
He saved us, not because of righteous things we
had done, but because of his mercy. He saved us
through the washing of rebirth and renewal by the
Holy Spirit

A New Heart
Deuteronomy 30:6
The LORD your God will circumcise your hearts and
the hearts of your descendants, so that you may love
him with all your heart and with all your soul, and
live.

Ezekiel 11:19
I will give them an undivided heart and put a new
spirit in them; I will remove from them their heart of
stone and give them a heart of flesh.

Ezekiel 36:26
I will give you a new heart and put a new spirit in
you; I will remove from you your heart of stone and
give you a heart of flesh.

Ezekiel 36:27
And I will put my Spirit in you and move you to follow
my decrees and be careful to keep my laws.

A New Creation
2 Corinthians 5:17-18
Therefore, if anyone is in Christ, he is a new creation;
the old has gone, the new has come! All this is from
God, who reconciled us to himself through Christ and
gave us the ministry of reconciliation:

Galatians 6:15
Neither circumcision nor uncircumcision means
anything; what counts is a new creation.

Ephesians 2:10
For we are God's workmanship, created in Christ
Jesus to do good works, which God prepared in
advance for us to do.

"No one..."

A Resurrection
John 5:21
For just as the Father raises the dead and gives them
life, even so the Son gives life to whom he is pleased
to give it.

John 11:14-15
So then he told them plainly, "Lazarus is dead, and
for your sake I am glad I was not there, so that you
may believe. But let us go to him."

John 11:38-44
Jesus, once more deeply moved, came to the tomb.
It was a cave with a stone laid across the entrance.
"Take away the stone," he said. "But, Lord," said
Martha, the sister of the dead man, "by this time there
is a bad odor, for he has been there four days." Then
Jesus said, "Did I not tell you that if you believed,
you would see the glory of God?" So they took away
the stone. Then Jesus looked up and said, "Father,
I thank you that you have heard me. I knew that
you always hear me, but I said this for the benefit of
the people standing here, that they may believe that
you sent me." When he had said this, Jesus called
in a loud voice, "Lazarus, come out!" The dead man
came out, his hands and feet wrapped with strips
of linen, and a cloth around his face. Jesus said to
them, "Take off the grave clothes and let him go."

Ephesians 2:1
As for you, you were dead in your transgressions and sins.

Ephesians 2:5
[God] made us alive with Christ even when we were
dead in transgressions – it is by grace you have been
saved.

Colossians 2:13
When you were dead in your sins and in the
uncircumcision of your sinful nature, God made you
alive with Christ. He forgave us all our sins.

A Gift

John 17:2

For you granted him authority over all people that he might give eternal life to all those you have given him.

1 Corinthians 4:7

For who makes you different from anyone else? What do you have that you did not receive? And if you did receive it, why do you boast as though you did not?

Ephesians 2:8-9

For it is by grace you have been saved, through faith – and this not from yourselves, it is the gift of God – not by works, so that no one can boast.

Acts 5:31

God exalted him to his own right hand as Prince and Savior that he might give repentance and forgiveness of sins to Israel.

Acts 11:18

When they heard this, they had no further objections and praised God, saying, "So then, God has granted even the Gentiles repentance unto life."

Acts 13:48

When the Gentiles heard this, they were glad and honored the word of the Lord; and all who were appointed for eternal life believed.

Acts 16:14

One of those listening was a woman named Lydia, a dealer in purple cloth from the city of Thyatira, who was a worshiper of God. The Lord opened her heart to respond to Paul's message.

Acts 18:27

When Apollos wanted to go to Achaia, the brothers encouraged him and wrote to the disciples there to welcome him. On arriving, he was a great help to those who by grace had believed.

Philippians 1:29
For it has been granted to you on behalf of Christ not only to believe on him, but also to suffer for him.

2 Timothy 2:25-26
Those who oppose him he must gently instruct, in the hope that God will grant them repentance leading them to a knowledge of the truth, and that they will come to their senses and escape from the trap of the devil, who has taken them captive to do his will.

V. Once saved, always saved – "the grandest thought in the Bible. Once you believe you can never be lost, you can never go to hell."[2]

SCRIPTURE PROOFS
Romans 8:29-30
For those God foreknew he also predestined to be conformed to the likeness of his Son, that he might be the firstborn among many brothers. And those he predestined, he also called; those he called, he also justified; those he justified, he also glorified.

Romans 8:35-39
Who shall separate us from the love of Christ? Shall trouble or hardship or persecution or famine or nakedness or danger or sword? As it is written: "For your sake we face death all day long; we are considered as sheep to be slaughtered." No, in all these things we are more than conquerors through him who loved us. For I am convinced that neither death nor life, neither angels nor demons, neither the present nor the future, nor any powers, neither height nor depth, nor anything else in all creation, will be able to separate us from the love of God that is in Christ Jesus our Lord.

1 Corinthians 1:8
He will keep you strong to the end, so that you will be blameless on the day of our Lord Jesus Christ.

Ephesians 1:5
He predestined us to be adopted as his sons through Jesus Christ, in accordance with his pleasure and will.

Ephesians 1:13-14
And you also were included in Christ when you heard the word of truth, the gospel of your salvation. Having believed, you were marked in him with a seal, the promised Holy Spirit, who is a deposit guaranteeing our inheritance until the redemption of those who are God's possession – to the praise of his glory.

Ephesians 4:30
And do not grieve the Holy Spirit of God, with whom you were sealed for the day of redemption.

Philippians 1:6
[I am] confident of this, that he who began a good work in you will carry it on to completion until the day of Christ Jesus.

1 Peter 1:3-5
Praise be to the God and Father of our LORD Jesus Christ! In his great mercy he has given us new birth into a living hope through the resurrection of Jesus Christ from the dead, and into an inheritance that can never perish, spoil or fade – kept in heaven for you, who through faith are shielded by God's power until the coming of the salvation that is ready to be revealed in the last time.

John 10:28
I give them eternal life, and they shall never perish; no one can snatch them out of my hand.

John 14:21
Whoever has my commands and obeys them, he is the one who loves me. He who loves me will be loved by my Father, and I too will love him and show myself to him.

John 15:1-11

I am the true vine, and my Father is the gardener. He cuts off every branch in me that bears no fruit, while every branch that does bear fruit he prunes so that it will be even more fruitful. You are already clean because of the word I have spoken to you. Remain in me, and I will remain in you. No branch can bear fruit by itself; it must remain in the vine. Neither can you bear fruit unless you remain in me. I am the vine; you are the branches. If a man remains in me and I in him, he will bear much fruit; apart from me you can do nothing. If anyone does not remain in me, he is like a branch that is thrown away and withers; such branches are picked up, thrown into the fire and burned. If you remain in me and my words remain in you, ask whatever you wish, and it will be given you. This is to my Father's glory, that you bear much fruit, showing yourselves to be my disciples. As the Father has loved me, so have I loved you. Now remain in my love. If you obey my commands, you will remain in my love, just as I have obeyed my Father's commands and remain in his love. I have told you this so that my joy may be in you and that your joy may be complete.

Ephesians 2:10

For we are God's workmanship, created in Christ Jesus to do good works, which God prepared in advance for us to do.

1 Peter 5:10

And the God of all grace, who called you to his eternal glory in Christ, after you have suffered a little while, will himself restore you and make you strong, firm and steadfast.

2 Peter 1:10

Therefore, my brothers, be all the more eager to make your calling and election sure. For if you do these things, you will never fall.

Philippians 2:12-13
Therefore, my dear friends, as you have always obeyed – not only in my presence, but now much more in my absence – continue to work out your salvation with fear and trembling, for it is God who works in you to will and to act according to his good purpose.

Philippians 3:12-15
Not that I have already obtained all this, or have already been made perfect, but I press on to take hold of that for which Christ Jesus took hold of me. Brothers, I do not consider myself yet to have taken hold of it. But one thing I do: Forgetting what is behind and straining toward what is ahead, I press on toward the goal to win the prize for which God has called me heavenward in Christ Jesus. All of us who are mature should take such a view of things. And if on some point you think differently, that too God will make clear to you.

1 John 3:9
No one who is born of God will continue to sin, because God's seed remains in him; he cannot go on sinning, because he has been born of God.

1 John 5:18
We know that anyone born of God does not continue to sin; the one who was born of God keeps him safe, and the evil one cannot harm him.

Hebrews 5:11-6:12
We have much to say about this, but it is hard to explain because you are slow to learn. In fact, though by this time you ought to be teachers, you need someone to teach you the elementary truths of God's word all over again. You need milk, not solid food! Anyone who lives on milk, being still an infant, is not acquainted with the teaching about righteousness. But solid food is for the mature, who by constant use have trained themselves to distinguish good from

evil. Therefore let us leave the elementary teachings about Christ and go on to maturity, not laying again the foundation of repentance from acts that lead to death, and of faith in God, instruction about baptisms, the laying on of hands, the resurrection of the dead, and eternal judgment. And God permitting, we will do so. It is impossible for those who have once been enlightened, who have tasted the heavenly gift, who have shared in the Holy Spirit, who have tasted the goodness of the word of God and the powers of the coming age, if they fall away, to be brought back to repentance, because to their loss they are crucifying the Son of God all over again and subjecting him to public disgrace. Land that drinks in the rain often falling on it and that produces a crop useful to those for whom it is farmed receives the blessing of God. But land that produces thorns and thistles is worthless and is in danger of being cursed. In the end it will be burned. Even though we speak like this, dear friends, we are confident of better things in your case – things that accompany salvation. God is not unjust; he will not forget your work and the love you have shown him as you have helped his people and continue to help them. We want each of you to show this same diligence to the very end, in order to make your hope sure. We do not want you to become lazy, but to imitate those who through faith and patience inherit what has been promised.

1 John 2:19
They went out from us, but they did not really belong to us. For if they had belonged to us, they would have remained with us; but their going showed that none of them belonged to us.

1 John 2:25
And this is what he promised us – even eternal life.

John 16:22b
...and no one will take away your joy.

ENDNOTES

1. For an exhaustive examination see: *The Westminster Confession of Faith* http://www.opc.org/documents/WCF_frames.html
2. Edwin H. Palmer, General Editor of the *NIV Study Bible*.

Appendix 3:
The Gospel in brief

You have just read the gospel in Jesus' own words.
It is my prayer that God has spoken to you through
these six brief, unequivocal declarations – six
unshakable certainties – from Jesus Christ, the Son
of God whose deeds demonstrated how much he
loves his chosen – "For God so loved the world ..."
(John 3:16). I hope you have summarized in your
own words and memorized the most important
lesson that can ever cross the mind of man. If
this has changed your life, if God has opened your
eyes and regenerated your heart, then share the
news with your friends. And I would love to hear
from you as well, that I too might rejoice with
the angels in heaven (Luke 15:7). If you were a
Christian before you read this, I pray that Jesus'
words have reinforced your conviction and inspired
you to share this greatest of all good news with
those you love who are unsaved.

Most everyone has a dear friend or family
member who does not know the Lord. Nothing is
harder than trying to witness to God's amazing
grace to a close friend or family member. It is so
stressful to confront a loved one with the error

of his ways that the mind tends to get flustered and the tongue tied, so make a manuscript and memorize it. God's Word is a stumbling block, a rock of offense (Romans 9:33) to those whose eyes have not been opened to see the kingdom of heaven, and our human nature does not want to offend our dearly loved ones. Yet our Puritan forebears understood that an unsaved person must be awakened to his grave peril before he is motivated to do something about it. Thus the "Great Awakening" of the seventeenth century led by Jonathan Edwards and George Whitefield and others. Once one understands how a merciful God has graciously made a way for a sinner to flee from the wrath to come – by the intellectual, heartfelt, soul-deep acceptance, through the inner working of the Holy Spirit, of the gift of faith in Him – a changed heart lives in overwhelming gratitude to God, and would love Him unreservedly even if there were no eternal hell.

Here is a brief gospel presentation in my words as an example. You may use it, adapt it to your needs, or create your own. It represents many hours of thought, trying to be as concise and clear as I can. And remember this as you strive to witness to those you love: A child of God is called to witness, in season and out (2 Tim. 4:2), and, as Jesus' statements make crystal clear in this little book, a sovereign God does the eye opening and heart changing. So witness as if your loved one's salvation depended on your words, and pray as if it depends on God, which it clearly does. May the God of infinite love bless your efforts, that they might reflect His glory.

A Personal Invitation from JD Wetterling

The rich young man asked Jesus, "What must I do to inherit eternal life?" (Mark 10:17, Luke 10:25). He made the same mistake so common today. He assumed he had to earn eternal life. You cannot physically do anything to inherit something. An inheritance comes from what has been done for you, and that is the heart of the gospel. The word means "good news," and surely it is the best good news you could ever hear. Nothing you do – your "works"– can earn you eternal life. Rather, the Bible says "you have been saved through faith... not [as] a result of works" (Eph. 2:8-9). The gospel is best summed up in Jesus' own words: "God so loved the world, that he gave his only Son, that whoever believes in him should not perish but have eternal life" (John 3:16).

Why should I perish? I am a good person, you say? What is so critical about believing in him who called himself the Son of God? I have never murdered anyone. I love my spouse and I have never been unfaithful, and I do better than most at keeping the Ten Commandments. Haven't you had those thoughts? Many think God grades our acts (our "works") on a curve and they have been good enough to get into heaven. Well, listen carefully. Jesus said anyone who is angry at his brother will get the same judgment as a murderer – the sixth commandment (Matt. 5:21-22a). Jesus also said, that "everyone who looks at a woman with lustful intent has already committed adultery with her in his heart" – the seventh commandment (Matt. 5:28). Loving anyone or anything more than God is a violation of the first commandment. And James said breaking one commandment is as bad as breaking them all (James 2:10). It is a sin, even if you break it only in your thoughts, and a single sin will keep you out of heaven. Pretty tough standard isn't it? That is the whole point. God wrote the Ten Commandments to make us painfully aware of how we have sinned against an infinitely Holy God. Paul told the Romans, "through the law comes knowledge of sin" (Romans 3:20). All mankind has been sinful since Adam and Eve were evicted from the garden of Eden for their sin (Gen. 3: 13-24). We are all sinners, and it is crucial that you know just how angry God is about sin. Jonathan Edwards describes it best in his famous sermon, *Sinners in the Hands of an Angry God*.

Lest you think Edwards had an outrageous flight of fancy when he preached that sermon, read the Son of God's own words. Jesus said, "If your right eye causes you to sin, tear it out and throw it away. For it is better that you lose one of your members than that your whole body be thrown into hell. And if your right hand causes you to sin, cut it off and throw it away. For it is better that you lose one of your members than that your whole body go into hell" (Matt. 5:29-30). He said if anyone causes a little child of God to sin, "it would be better for him to have a great millstone fastened around his neck and to be drowned in the depth of the sea," than to suffer the eternal judgment that awaits him (Matt. 18:6). Dear one, do I have your attention? This is the most important issue of your life. Awful wrath, incomprehensible terrors await anyone who dies in his sin. But an infinitely holy and loving God has provided the most amazing remedy in the gospel nutshell of John 3:16. "God so loved the world, that he gave his only Son, that whoever believes in him should not perish but have eternal life."

It really is as simple as it sounds. Belief gets you eternal life – you do not and cannot earn it. You can never make yourself perfect enough to meet heaven's holiness requirements. So what does "believe in him" mean? It means (1) believe Jesus Christ was who he said he was, the Son of God, come to earth as a man, just as the Bible states; (2) believe that, in the greatest act of love that ever was, he died on the cross to pay the penalty for your sins, and (3) believe that he rose from the dead, to live forever in heaven with all who believe in him. Paul said, "if you confess with your mouth that Jesus is Lord and believe in your heart that God raised him from the dead, you will be saved" (Romans 10:9). Without this belief you will not go to heaven. You will "perish" – be sentenced to eternity in hell (Matt. 12:30-32, 5:29-30, 10:28).

Now here is the really amazing part of this good news: God gives you this belief (Romans 8:28-30), an inheritance beyond measure! "For by grace you have been saved through faith. And this is not your own doing; it is the gift of God, not a result of works" (Eph. 2:8). "Grace" is commonly defined as "unmerited favor," but it is much more than that. It is God's mercy showered upon one who deserves his wrath. "Saved" means salvation from the eternal punishment your sins deserve. "Faith" is not just intellectual agreement with a theory, but trust in a living person – Jesus Christ who, in His great love, died to pay for your sins. "Not as a result of works" means nothing you do on your own saves you or even leads you to faith – God changes your heart and inclines your will (or put another way, God enables you). Salvation is God's sovereign work, not something a sinner does for himself. Good works are the fruit of the Holy Spirit dwelling in true believers (Gal. 5:22) and a grateful response to God's grace. As acts of your gratitude they glorify God, but they do not earn you salvation.

Paul explains the absolute necessity of God's grace: "There is no one who understands, no one who seeks God" (Romans 3:11) on his own. But in his amazing grace, "God...works in you, both to will and to work for his good pleasure" (Phil. 2:13). God opens your eyes to your sins of commission and omission, and inclines your will to repent of them – to be sincerely sorry for and ask God's forgiveness for breaking his laws, that is, the Ten Commandments and the myriad variations of them in deed and word and even thought. And to live in grateful, humble acceptance and total reliance on his grace and mercy. Sound impossible? It is – for man by his own efforts, but Jesus said, "What is impossible with men is possible with God" (Luke 18:27). Believers are forgiven sinners! They are redeemed! Redemption – the salvation of your soul unto eternal glory – is the work of God through Christ from first to last. As John the Baptist said, "A person cannot receive even one thing unless it is given him from heaven" (John 3:27). And James said, "Every good gift...[comes] down from the Father" (James 1:17).

Jesus told the woman at the well that if you know God's amazing gift, ask and he will give (John 4:10). Notice there is nothing conditional between asking and receiving, once God has opened your eyes to the availability of his free gift.

This is the gospel, the good news of God's grace, his free gift of everlasting life with him, and that is as good as good news can get!

Oh sinner, think about the fearful danger you are in. For the sake of your eternal soul, prayerfully ask God to open your eyes to His truth, change your heart, give you faith in Christ's work on your behalf, and enable you to fervently seek repentance and live in humble trust in Him alone. Your security and joy will be guaranteed by the highest authority: Jesus said, "No one" can snatch you out of his hand, and "No one will take away your joy." Do it now. You know not the day nor the hour of your death or Christ's return.

About the Author

JD Wetterling is an ordained elder and deacon in the Presbyterian Church in America and Resident Manager of Ridge Haven, the Presbyterian Church in America's (PCA) Conference and Retreat Center in the Blue Ridge Mountains of North Carolina (www.ridgehaven.org).

He is the author of *Son of Thunder*, a novel based on his experiences as a fighter pilot in Vietnam, and numerous op-ed columns and essays in America's largest periodicals. His speaking credits include Presbyterian pulpits, radio, TV and varied audiences across North America.

Learn more about him and his work at www.jdwetterling.com.

Other Books of Interest from
Christian Focus Publications

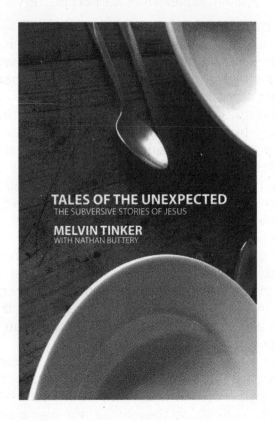

TALES OF THE UNEXPECTED
THE SUBVERSIVE STORIES OF JESUS

MELVIN TINKER
WITH NATHAN BUTTERY

Tales of the Unexpected

The Surprising Stories of Jesus of Nazareth

Melvin Tinker with Nathan Buttery

At Christmas time whilst singing carols about 'gentle Jesus, meek and mild' we can miss that this time-dividing man had an edge about what he had to say. His parables are sometimes not 'nice spiritual stories'.

They capture the imagination, they paint timeless pictures, but they are also more than that. When you read, you get the unnerving sense that through them Jesus can see right through you. They can be unsettling, challenging, able to change you - that the sense of shame and lost-ness that we often feel, may be provided with answers in what he has to say.

The Parable was an unusual form of teaching to Jesus' hearers, the Old Testament has only one main example, yet one third of Jesus' recorded words in the New Testament are parables. If these stories were so important to him, they should also be important to us.

Jesus was a communications genius, his parables convey important spiritual truths – appealing to young and old, rich and poor, educated and non-educated – because they are a not just a story to be understood, they are a spiritual temperature gauge.

Melvin Tinker is the Vicar of St. John's Church of England, Newlands, Hull. A popular author on culture and faith.

ISBN 1-84550-116-0

PRAYING
THE SAVIOUR'S WAY

LET JESUS' PRAYER RESHAPE YOUR PRAYER LIFE

DEREK THOMAS

Praying the Saviour's Way

Let Jesus' Prayer Reshape your Prayer Life

Derek Thomas

Even in today's post Christian society the Lord's Prayer remains widely known. Its beauty is that it can be understood by a child, but has tremendously profound lessons for those of us who investigate it more deeply. However, our tendency is to allow familiarity to breed complacency. We can repeat the Lord's Prayer verbatim, but do we ponder its message and follow its example?

In his refreshing and lively style Derek Thomas brings us back to the Lord's Prayer and helps us to re-examine it. With penetrating accuracy Thomas considers the Lord's Prayer and shows how it is a clear guide to that most vital component of our spiritual health - our prayer life.

'Thomas has given us an insightful and inspiring look at the Lord's Prayer. The church has always returned to Christ's instruction on prayer to form prayers that are pleasing to God. In our day when new forms of spirituality are appearing all around us, we need to return once again.'

Richard L. Pratt, Jr.,
Reformed Theological Seminary, Orlando, Florida

'Instructive, practical, readable, challenging. Each chapter will make you eager for the next course. Nourishing fare indeed!'

Sinclair B. Ferguson,
First Presbyterian Church, Columbia, South Carolina

Derek Thomas is Professor of Systematic Theology at the Reformed Theological Seminary, Jackson, Mississippi.

ISBN 1-85792-696-X

Christian Focus Publications

publishes books for all ages

Our mission statement –

STAYING FAITHFUL

In dependence upon God we seek to help make His infallible Word, the Bible, relevant. Our aim is to ensure that the Lord Jesus Christ is presented as the only hope to obtain forgiveness of sin, live a useful life and look forward to heaven with Him.

REACHING OUT

Christ's last command requires us to reach out to our world with His gospel. We seek to help fulfill that by publishing books that point people towards Jesus and help them develop a Christ-like maturity. We aim to equip all levels of readers for life, work, ministry and mission.

Books in our adult range are published in three imprints.

Christian Focus contains popular works including biographies, commentaries, basic doctrine and Christian living. Our children's books are also published in this imprint.

Mentor focuses on books written at a level suitable for Bible College and seminary students, pastors, and other serious readers. The imprint includes commentaries, doctrinal studies, examination of current issues and church history.

Christian Heritage contains classic writings from the past.

Christian Focus Publications, Ltd
Geanies House, Fearn,
Ross-shire, IV20 1TW, Scotland, United Kingdom
info@christianfocus.com

For details of our titles visit us on our website
www.christianfocus.com